A Designer's Log
Case Studies in Instructional Design

A Designer's Log
Case Studies in Instructional Design

by Michael Power

AU PRESS

© 2009 Michael Power
Second printing 2010

Published by AU Press, Athabasca University
1200, 10011 – 109 Street
Edmonton, AB T5J 3S8

A volume in the Issues in Distance Education series,
edited by Terry Anderson, Ph.D.
ISSN 1919-4382 Issues in Distance Education Series (Print)
ISSN 1919-4390 Issues in Distance Education Series (Online)

Library and Archives Canada Cataloguing in Publication

Power, Michael
A designer's log : case studies in instructional design / by Michael Power.

Translation of: Le conseiller pédagogique réflexif.
Includes bibliographical references.
ISBN 978-1-897425-61-9 (Print)
ISBN 978-1-897425-46-6 (Electronic)

1. Universities and colleges--Curricula--Planning. 2. Instructional
systems--Design. 3. Curriculum planning. 4. Universities and
colleges--Curricula--Planning--Case studies. 5. Distance education.
I. Title.

LB2361.P6813 2009   378.1'99   C2009-904552-4

Printed and bound in Canada by Marquis Book Printing

I wish to thank Dr. Claire Lapointe, Université Laval, for her unwavering support and her critical appraisal of this project as it evolved from a need, to a desire, to an idea and finally to an actual book. I'd also like to recognize Professor Bernard Nadeau from Université de Moncton who, over the years, has been a stalwart friend in need/indeed and an educator with a flair for intuition. Finally, this book would have never seen print without the unconditional support from my friend and colleague Dr. David Kaufman of Simon Fraser University.

- Michael Power

Contents

Foreword

The transformation of a traditional learning institution into a dual-mode institution offering courses on-campus as well as online is not a task for the faint at heart. What has to be appreciated is that subject matter experts, used to teaching in a classroom, face a daunting challenge when requested to teach at a distance or online. Indeed, only a few have ever systematically planned their courses. Yet systematic planning is just what is needed to be a successful teacher.

To implement online learning in a traditional institution, we have to adopt a design model which is both easy to understand and easy to use, namely because faculty generally do not have a lot of time to dedicate to this task. In this book, the course design model proposed by Dr. Power is flexible and represents an important step in making course design both doable and affordable.

There are a lot of course design models out there but I have to admit that there are very few that are as easy to use as that presented by the author. What makes this model truly original is that it involves close interaction between the subject matter expert (professor) and the instructional designer (ID). What I find of particular interest is that it involves the ID planning a course directly online with the professor at his/her side and implementing existing and relevant elements of the professor's on-campus course. The ten case studies presented in Dr.

Power's book amply demonstrate this "faculty-based practices" approach indicative of his model.

Books dealing with instructional design usually propose a theoretical model and include a few examples to demonstrate applicability. Dr. Power, however, has chosen to present actual case studies demonstrating practices that work, and then adds theoretical underpinnings. That is, I believe, what is of greatest interest in this book. The cases presented, being very detailed, actually walk us through just what happened and how it happened. That is why I think that this book will be exceptionally useful to anyone working in this area. In this regard, the contribution the author has made to the general field of instructional design is important.

Instructional designer culture is not limited to theoretical knowledge or design-related skills alone. They must acquire and demonstrate mastery of specific and requisite interpersonal skills and attitudes that many of us tend to gloss over. This is yet another strong point of this book; I am particularly impressed by the flexibility shown by the author in dealing with the various professors he encountered. Possessing such skills and attitudes or not can often make all the difference between the success of the failure of an instructional design project for online learning. By reading this book, I'm confident that both practicing and future instructional designers will understand the importance of tact and attitudes de tolerance and tenacity, attributes which are so important when dealing with subject matter experts.

Moreover, I'm convinced that these case studies presented by Dr. Power will not only be useful to instructional designers who use his model to design online courses but to all instructional designers in whatever they design. As a matter of fact, I observed that several of the cases described by the author refer to many frequently encountered problems in instructional design.

It is therefore with great pleasure that I recommend Dr. Power's book to all those who are interested in course design and, particularly, in online course design in dual-mode universities.

Dr. Robert Brien
Laval University
Quebec City

Preface

"The first was never to accept anything for true which I did not clearly know to be such; that is to say, carefully to avoid precipitancy and prejudice, and to comprise nothing more in my judgement than what was presented to my mind so clearly and distinctly as to exclude all ground of doubt."

Excerpt from *Discours sur la méthode* by René Descartes

I first read the *Discours sur la méthode* when I was a community college student and I have to admit that, at the time, it did not have much of an effect. But over time, in the way a constant drip can erode even the hardest granite, it came to permeate my thinking. What Descartes said, in just a few words, seems to me to be the core of the scientific method, as it is based on the surest of foundations, the personal observation of phenomena. To my mind, Descartes lays the responsibility of seeing with our own eyes and hearing with our own ears, each and every one of us. To doubt is a reflex, the lack of which would imperil any scientific pursuit. Of course this does not mean that one should automatically reject what someone is telling us. Certainly not. But it does not mean we should accept it at face value either. A state of wariness is, I believe, permanently warranted, the duty to question one's understanding of a phenomenon, as well as that of others, is a ceaseless task.

Now that I have brazenly attempted to associate myself with one of science's brightest lights, please allow me to explain how this modest manuscript has the least to do with the monumental work of our august predecessor. When I began the research study on developing an appropriate dual-mode design model documented in the present log, I thought I had the world by the tail. I had over 12 years' experience in the field of instructional design in higher education, plus excellent instruction during my studies toward a Master's degree, as well as all the resources I thought I needed to complete the project at hand. I really could not see any difficulty, not a cloud on my horizon. It was thus, head-first and with a mind full of misplaced certitude, I undertook this journey of designing courses, first for distance education and subsequently for online learning.

It was not long before I started to see that all was not right with my world. Actually applying the instructional design theories I had diligently learned in graduate school when I began working with subject matter experts (SMEs) was harder than I could have imagined. In the field, I was confronted with design challenges of the like I had never before experienced. I found myself asking "What (on earth) can I base this or that design-related decision on?" The illustrious ADDIE approach, upon which is based a huge segment of design literature (Gustafson & Branch, 1997) was, surprisingly, of little or no use to me. I felt like I had just landed on a new planet without a map and without knowing the language of the inhabitants. Man, what a surprise! It was precisely then that Descartes' famous words started ringing in my ears and it seemed that I truly understood them for the first time: *"de ne recevoir jamais aucune chose pour vraie que je ne la connusse évidemment être telle"* (never to accept anything for true which I did not clearly know to be such).

Another author, more of a contemporary, came to mind to console me: Donald Schön. In a passage from his celebrated book *Educating the Reflexive Practitioner* quoted below, "The Crisis of Confidence in Professional Knowledge," he uses the analogy of solid versus swampy ground, that is, ground where we feel confident in what is under our feet in contrast to ground where we feel decidedly queasy.

In the varied topography of professional practice, there is a high, hard ground overlooking a swamp. On the high ground, manageable problems lend themselves to solution through the application of research-based theory and technique. In the swampy lowland, messy, confusing problems defy technical solution. The irony of this situation is that the problems of the high ground tend to be relatively unimportant to individuals or society at large, however great their technical interest may be, while in the swamp lie the problems of greatest human concern. The practitioner must choose. Shall he remain on the high ground where he can solve relatively unimportant problems according to the prevailing standards of rigor, or shall he descend to the swamp of important problems and nonrigorous inquiry?

He is, of course, alluding to the comfort of our carefully-nursed certitudes and well-ensconced traditions, as opposed to the swamp where problems are hard to define but oh so important for society. Then, he asks the million-dollar question: should a practitioner remain on the safe "high ground" or dare to venture below? That choice really hit me. During my research study, I felt rather lonely in the swamp. In a field of practice where there was little lighting and few guideposts, the idea of this book began to come together. Without the time needed for a thorough job, I felt I should at least attempt to chart a course for others to follow, without being overly self-critical of my accuracy in drawing the map. I consoled myself by thinking that, for anyone starting out on a journey, a rough map is better than no map at all.

Contrary to my preconceptions, there was not much in the literature to guide me in developing an appropriate design model for faculty moving from an on-campus teaching paradigm to an online learning paradigm. Anne-Marie Armstrong's thoroughly enjoyable edited collection about the experiences of designers in the corporate world wasn't yet available when I started this project. So that is how this book got started, as a real-life response to a problem I was experiencing. In essence, it is composed of notes I took while I working with subject matter experts who were intent on offering their courses at a distance and/or online.

Finally, I wish to recognize Valerie Clifford (2004) for an inspiring book review in which she addresses the question "Why should we keep a logbook?" She explains the necessity of documenting our life experiences as a guide to others: "When we tell stories, we express ourselves and learn from discussing our experience with others who may raise alternative views, suggest imaginative possibilities, and ask stimulating questions" (p. 63).

It is my sincere hope that my story as an ID (instructional designer) coming to terms with new and difficult problems and seeking solutions for them through a process of reflection, induction and deduction will be useful to other instructional designers, educational developers, faculty and administrators who are involved in distance education and online learning.

Dr. Michael Power
Quebec City
November 28, 2008

Introduction

This book deals with the design of distance education at an emerging dual-mode university, that is, a university offering courses both on-campus and via distance education or online in a variety of manners. It was written from the point of view of an instructional designer (ID) working alongside university professors in designing their courses for distance delivery.[1] It originated as my logbook, which I kept over a period of three years and in which I relate the ups and downs as well as the dos and don'ts of designing learning materials for students studying at a distance. It introduces you to ten faculty members with whom I shared this experience and lifts the veil on a seldom-reported, essentially undocumented, working environment.

Before presenting the cases, I will outline the underlying research study as well as introduce the design model that served as my original design prototype.

The Instructional Design Model Prototype

When I began a new mandate as instructional designer-researcher at an emerging dual-mode university, my main task was to accompany faculty members in readying their courses for distance delivery. Coming from a professional background of distance education in the single-mode tradition (such as The Open University in the United Kingdom), I was used to employing a highly structured design model with faculty members whose principal job was to create new courses or to revise existing ones. The model was industrial in nature and based on the division of labour, i.e. faculty and specialized professionals working as course teams. I had no inkling of how different my work would be in what was essentially a traditional university environment, albeit one with numerous distance education course offerings.

Indeed, I discovered the prevailing role of faculty in a traditional university to be quite different from the dominant role of faculty in single-mode distance education universities. First of all, traditional "on-campus" faculty, for the most part, have little understanding of what is involved in developing courses for distance education, let alone online learning (Twigg, 2002). Secondly, the traditional university structure is such that faculty do not benefit from the level of pedagogical and technical support inherent in the distance education approach to course design and development (Mortera-Gutierrez, 2002; Rumble & Harry, 1982). Moreover, although faculty in distance education universities conduct research which is essentially well received by their academic communities, in traditional universities the primacy of research over teaching is even more apparent (Maeroff, 2003). These are but some of the differences between the two milieus that have an immediate and profound impact on the amount of time faculty in traditional universities are willing and able to devote to planning their teaching.

Upon my entry into this dual-mode university environment, I began to realize that I could not simply go about my business as usual. Given these new circumstances, I had to find ways of fulfilling my mandate successfully. As I started working closely with faculty, it dawned on me that there was not a lot of literature available to instructional designers working in traditional universities. Indeed, according to Reiser (2001) "instructional design had little impact in higher education" (p. 62). I realized how true these words rang. For decades, the instructional design model, often simply referred to by the acronym ADDIE (each letter representing a step in the process: Analysis-Design-Development-Implementation-Evaluation), had been the paradigm guiding instructional design. Originally conceived during the Second World War as a means to train approximately eighteen million soldiers for theatres in Europe and the South Pacific, it was subsequently adopted by big business to staff American post-war industry. But it was not designed for the needs of higher education, which aims to develop the individual, one mind at a time, not vast numbers of warriors or employees. Therein lays the difference, and the rub. As important as it is to raise the skills level of the GI to an acceptable threshold to better his chances of surviving on the battlefield, it is equally important for society that universities hone the unique and diverse skills of gifted individuals capable of enlightening humanity with innovation, discovery and erudition. It is therefore no surprise that the university milieu has, by and large, been extraordinarily resistant to any attempt at industrializing its methods, approaches or practices (Moore & Kearsley, 2004). That instructional design has become equated, at least in the minds of some (Carr-Chellman, 2005; Magnussen, 2005), with a form of insidious influence geared to mass produce educational outcomes must be recognized as a failure of the ID field and its proponents to establish its relevance and clearly reveal its usefulness to a critical and discerning population.

Instructional design in an on-campus setting

In light of these preliminary remarks, it should be clear that my first major task was to figure out just how to go about accompanying faculty involved in distance education at a transitioning dual-mode university. This task prompted my first efforts to establish a working instructional design model that would produce acceptable results in this particular setting, given the available resources and despite its numerous limits.

Despite the fact that Reiser (2001) states, correctly I believe, that instructional design has had little impact on higher education, it would be untrue to say that there is no course planning occurring in higher education. Indeed, every faculty member spends an untold number of hours every term planning his or her courses, generally according to a firmly-anchored, discipline-based course planning tradition, in some cases stretching back centuries to the oldest universities of Europe. However, as much as tradition once played the main role in deciding and defining what would be taught and how it would be taught, currently research is increasingly filling that role. Nonetheless, although tradition is losing ground with regard to *what* is taught, it still seems to have a stranglehold on *how* it is taught.

It should therefore come as no surprise to the instructional designer that he or she will encounter resistance when attempting to carry out his/her role. But it does. University administrators began hiring substantial numbers of instructional designers in the 1980s and even more so in the 1990s and early 2000s to leverage new technology in the hopes of making distance education profitable for even the smallest universities. As the Internet and the Web proved to be even more enticing as a means to growth and as online learning became a reality, more IDs were added to staff in recognition of their knowledge and skills in creating learning environments for off-campus learners. Instructional designers, trained according to rigorous design models, started to see that they had been plunged into a hostile environment. Their solution: work with the early adopters, develop courses in niche fields, manage the process to respond to obvious needs while attempting to avoid conflict. This was my initial understanding of my new setting when I first embarked upon my new mandate. I knew it would require time and patience to make a dent in the status quo. I also knew I needed the proper tools with which to start my work.

The Prototype Development Process

Here, I will provide a synthesis of the process by which the initial instructional design model prototype emerged, the full version being available online (Power, 2005; Power 2008c). This study took place in a Francophone university in Canada where two main influences have been felt in the field of instructional design. Brien's *Design pédagogique*, (1992) an adaptation of Gagné & Briggs (1973) model, has become a classic work of reference for all levels of education in the Quebec educational system. *Design pédagogique* united the strength and relevance of the Gagne & Briggs model and adapted it to the needs of one of the fastest-developing educational systems of the twentieth century. Another book of reference was Prégent's (1990) *La préparation d'un cours [Charting Your Course]*, which was widely disseminated in universities throughout Québec and la Francophonie.[2] Prégent also bases his approach on Gagné (1985) as well as on Brien (1992) in identifying the course design-related tasks carried out by all professors.

This prototype was based on several sources other than those mentioned above, among which figure the ADDIE model as developed by Gagné (1985), Gagné & Briggs (1973), Gagné, Briggs & Wagner, (1992), Dick & Carey (2000), Dick, Carey & Carey (2007), Merrill (2002) and Reigeluth (1999), all highly representative of fundamental instructional design literature. Other sources include Otto Peter's (1983) industrial approach to distance education, Nipper's (1989) generations of distance education and Moore's (1993) well-known transactional distance theory. Previous work that I conducted on the congruency principle (Power, 1987, 1996; 2008b; 2008c) has also been influential in the development of the design prototype, as well as observations from the field I have gleaned from over thirty years in higher education, as a student, as a teaching assistant, as a research assistant, as an analyst, as a consultant, as an instructional designer/researcher and finally as a professor and an administrator. My varied experience allowed me to analyse faculty course planning techniques and practices, the results of which were reinvested in the initial instructional design model prototype.

My challenge was thus to bring together these diverse sources and hammer out a prototype that would allow me to assist faculty in successfully developing their courses for distance education. I therefore began by identifying "design phases" that professors would readily recognize as being similar to course planning phases prevalent in their fields. I intentionally made choices about which phases best represented the design pattern I felt they would find most useful in completing their task, in light of conditions (namely available resources and set limits) and predispositions I encountered. Based on the above theory-based instructional design conceptual framework, actual faculty course planning practices and following a comparative phases analysis, the following design phases were retained for the initial course design prototype as being theoretically sound and representative of actual faculty design practice at the dual-mode university in question:

1. *Analysis* (student needs assessment, course & program requirements as well as faculty interests, etc.)
2. *Module-Building* (Web-based course-related resource material, e.g. readings, etc.)
3. *Teaching Activities Development* (in-class exercises)
4. *Learner Support Activities Development* (additional, individualized resources for purposes of formative evaluation)

5. *Evaluation Instruments Development* (various testing instruments for purposes of summative evaluation)
6. *Items for Ongoing Improvement* (the "wish list," e.g. course resources, etc. to be developed later)

It was thus with this overall design model that my study began.

Notes

1. At the time of this study, there was a fair degree of ambiguity with regard to distance education and how it intersected with online learning and e-learning. It is my position that these terms identify differences mainly in technological issues and delivery systems which, as a trend, are becoming increasingly sophisticated, ubiquitous and learner-centered. For that reason, the reader will notice, towards the latter part of this book, my marked preference for the term "online learning" as I believe it accurately reflects technological changes occurring in the field.

2. For instance, Prégent's book was distributed to all new professors upon their arrival at the university where this study was conducted.

The Case Studies

Introduction to the case studies

The following ten case studies represent the first professors (also called subject matter experts or SMEs), out of a total of forty-four faculty members, to have implemented the instructional design model prototype (hereafter simply called the "model") at the university where the study was conducted. As the design work took place over a period of roughly three years, lessons learned during the design process of the first courses served to gradually transform the model as other professors participated in the design (or redesign) process of their courses. The model was thereby validated through actual user experience in the field. Modifications were made to anchor the model in the current and complex realities of academic life in an emerging dual-mode university.

NB. As I advance through each case study, I stop to reflect on various "critical incidents" (Flanagan, 1954) as they occur. Entitled *Meta-reflections*, you will find them in the order they arose during my working sessions for that case, in boxes such as the one below.

Meta-reflections

The content in these sections are in *italics*, drawn from entries I made in my logbook during the progress of my work with professors. Immediately after each session, I'd write up a report on items covered, decisions made, and so on, and expand on any notes I'd jotted down.

The demographic and professional characteristics of individual faculty members

Sample selection and faculty characteristics

Sample selection was based on faculty meeting the following criteria:
- they were full-time professors at an emerging dual-mode university;
- they were all in Humanities (Education, Music, Languages, Law);
- they were preparing one of their courses for off-campus delivery and
- they agreed to implement the proposed instructional design model prototype (henceforth, the "model").

Various characteristics of the ten faculty members who participated in this study were identified as being highly descriptive of the context of this study (see Table 1). They were of several types: demographic (gender), career-related (professorial rank), participant-related (motivation), circumstance-related (time-to-delivery, i.e. time allotted for course design before course delivery) and knowledge-related (degree of familiarity with instructional design principles and distance education practices) and finally course-related (current general and specific objectives development level). (See Table 1)

Table 1. Characteristics of the population sample

1. **Gender**: M / F

2. **Academic Rank**:
    AST = Assistant
    ASC = Associate
    FP = Full professor

3. **Reason for participating in the design process**:
    O = organizational
    P = personal

4. **Time-to-delivery**:
    1 = course already begun or is about to begin
    2 = beginning in between 2 and 4 months
    3 = beginning in more than 4 months

5. **Availability**: Total faculty availability in hours
      1 = between 1 and 15 hours
      2 = between 16 and 30 hours
      3 = between 31 and 45 hours
      4 = more than 46 hours

6. **Number of sessions**: Number of working sessions between designer and faculty member
      (between 1 and 8+)

7. **Knowledge of Instructional Design**: Faculty knowledge levels
      1 = novice level
      2 = intermediate level
      3 = advanced level

8. **Knowledge of Distance Education**: Faculty knowledge levels
      1 = no knowledge of DE
      2 = taught one or two DE courses
      3 = taught three or more DE courses

9. **General Objectives & Specific Objectives** development level
      1 = no objectives
      2 = only GOs
      3 = GOs + SOs (limited number of SOs) taught three or more DE courses

Table 2. Synthesis of population sample characteristics on a case-by-case basis

	Characteristics	Cases									
		1	2	3	4	5	6	7	8	9	10
1	Gender	M	F	F	F	F	M	M	M	M	F
2	Academic Rank	AST	AST	AST	ASC	ASC	FP	FP	FP	ASC	ASC
3	Reason	O	O	O	O	O	O	P	P	O	P
4	Time-to-delivery	2	1	2	1	1	2	3	3	3	3
5	Availability	1	1	1	1	1	3	4	3	3	2
6	Number of sessions	6	4	7	5	6	8+	8	8+	8+	7
7	Knowledge of Design	1	1	1	3	2	2	1	1	1	1
8	Knowledge of DE	1	1	1	2	1	2	1	1	1	1
9	Objectives (GO/SO)	2	2	3	2	3	1	3	2	2	3

In a nutshell, actual faculty characteristics broke down in the following ways:

1. *Gender*: Five males and five females
2. *Academic rank*: Three Assistant, four Associate and three Full Professors
3. *Reason* (for becoming involved): Seven were organizationally motivated, three were personally motivated
4. *Availability*: Five were minimally available (1–15 hours), one was slightly more available (16–30 hours), three were relatively available (31–45 hours) and one was very available (more than 46 hours)
5. *Number of* (working) *sessions*: An average of 6.7 per faculty member
6. *Time-to-delivery*: Three had a month or less to prepare their courses; three had 2–4 months and four had more than 4 months
7. *Knowledge of instructional design (ID) principles*: Seven knew little of ID
8. *Knowledge of distance education (DE)*: Eight had no experience with DE
9. *Objectives development level*: only one had no objectives whatsoever; five had main objectives only.

CASE STUDY 1
WALKING THE WALK

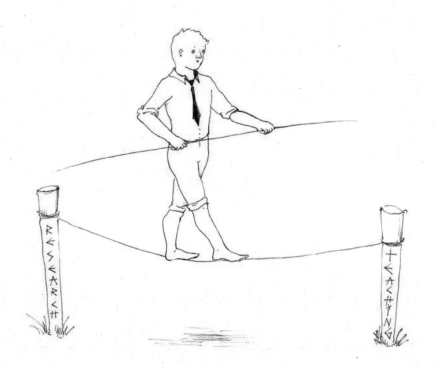

Case Characteristics

Table 3: Characteristics of the subject matter expert

Gender	Rank	Reason	Time	Availability	No. of sessions	K/ Design	K/ DE	GO/ SO
M	AST	O	1	1	6	1	1	2

Gender: male

Rank: AST = assistant

Reason: O = organisational

Time-to-delivery:

  2 = beginning in between 2 to 4 months

Availability: 1 = minimally available (1-15 hrs)

Number of sessions = 6

Knowledge of Design 1 = low level

Knowledge of DE: 1 = has never offered

  distance courses

General Obj. /Specific Obj.: 2 = GOs only

As the above table indicates, the first case study involved a male, Assistant Professor who was designing his course for organizational (O) purposes. His course would be starting in about four months and the time he had to devote to this work was quite limited (1). Indeed, as it turned out, we met only seven (7) times. Finally, his knowledge of instructional design was rudimentary, as was his knowledge of distance education. He had developed only general objectives (GOs).

The professor had taught this course only once before and he had done so on campus, while other professors before him had taught the same course using videoconferencing. His Department Head and Programs Director decided that the program of which this course was a component was to be offered at a distance, to groups of students distributed among several sites. They wished to continue basing this course around a weekly videoconference but wanted to complete the session by other didactic means, such as e-mail and a new Learning Management System (LMS) that the University had just adopted. Because the course would be taught over the next term, the professor had only three to four months to prepare his course.

Before our first meeting, I asked the professor to email me a copy of his current course syllabus and, furthermore, I invited him to go to my website so that he could view two presentations found there, "the congruency principle"[1] and the steps in the design prototype model (presented above) that I had developed to support faculty in designing their courses.

Session 1: At the very beginning of our first meeting, I decided that, despite the fact that we were working under conditions that bespoke the very essence of urgency, it was appropriate to avoid getting off to a flying start. Rather, I started off by describing who I was (an instructional designer) and what I did (ISD). I followed up by asking him if he had seen the presentations, which he had. He didn't have any specific questions about them but he did, however, mention his apprehension of the scale of the work to be undertaken and of the small amount of time in which to do it. He was worried because he felt the proposed model was relatively demanding and because he had only about forty hours overall to dedicate to designing his course. I then explained the concept of varying levels of design and production (or "layers of necessity," as Tessmer & Wedman [1990] put it) and the "process of ongoing improvement" of his course, which seemed to reassure him.

Having already read over his syllabus, I then asked him to talk to me about his course: whether he enjoyed teaching it, what it was that he liked about it, why he felt it was important to his students, how it fit into the program, how it was regarded by his colleagues, the extent to which it had been planned in conjunction with the other courses (earlier or later) in the program and, finally, whether there was public interest in his course (from a social relevance standpoint). By freely discussing his course, I hoped the professor would become sufficiently motivated to effectively start the design process.

I find it is important, during the first meeting, to outline my role as instructional designer in the design of a course. I have come to understand that only a few professors have ever heard of ISD and that, consequently, it is important to take the time to explain to them what exactly designers do (and don't do...), thereby allowing them to set reasonable expectations. Taking time, at the outset, to exchange informally with faculty members on his or her course has, in my experience, proven to be time well spent, especially as the ID and the Subject Matter Expert (faculty member) initiate a common project which may require months, even up to a year, of close collaboration. In my experience, sharing perspectives on the upcoming course to be designed, creating an emotional bond – a feeling of trust – is crucial at this point. Not only must the faculty member understand what the ID does, they also have to feel that the designer and the technical team are behind them 100 percent, ready to guide and support them throughout the entire process. Otherwise, faculty are usually (and understandably) not very keen to dedicate their valuable time and significant effort to this work which, for the most part, is often disregarded when they are assessed for tenure or promotion. Consequently, low-level motivation among faculty for design usually translates into a loose commitment to the project and, sometimes, into a sudden halt in the process before it is completed. Understanding to what degree faculty are motivated allows me, the designer, to have realistic course design objectives that set the bar just high enough to advance the process towards an optimal point while not so high as to discourage faculty and doom the process.

As we worked our way through the design process, I realized that it was all about finding balance, being realistic and in tune with faculty needs and expectations.

Telling me about his course in broad terms, he said it occupied a central position in the program and that the course objectives were quite different from those in the other courses of the program. According to him, there was no redundancy or repetition. I followed up, however, on this latter point by asking if he had ever checked his colleagues' syllabi for duplication of objectives, to which he replied "No, never," adding that he did not know exactly what objectives had been set for the courses taught by his colleagues. We parted with his agreeing to obtain and study his colleagues' syllabi before our next session.

The fact that this professor was not at all aware of what his colleagues were teaching did not surprise me. In my experience, faculty, especially the newly-hired, are generally so busy in their escalating multi-tasking (research-teaching-service) that they simply don't have the time to fully acquaint themselves with their colleagues' syllabi. Nevertheless, as an ID, I find it extremely important that such an analysis take place to avoid redundancy, which can be so detrimental to student motivation and, ultimately, achievement.

Session 2: I began this session by asking the professor if he had had time to analyse his colleagues' syllabi. He had not but promised to do so before our next meeting. We returned to the study of his syllabus, which turned out to be a relatively typical one, containing the usual information, such as the purpose and description of the course, the professor's contact information, a series of general objectives, subjects or contents divided into units, evaluation guidelines and a bibliography. The general objectives were loosely grouped in a list and were neither linked to the contents nor the evaluation guidelines. Moreover, there was no mention of a course schedule, i.e. the chronological progress through material in the course. I noticed that he envisaged covering a considerable number of case studies, which would to require the students to read about a hundred pages a week. When I asked him if he had difficulty in getting through all that material the last time he taught this course, he told me he had. He added that, towards the end of the course, there were cases he couldn't cover due to a lack of time.

Initially, our discussions focused principally on his general objectives. We distributed these objectives throughout the fifteen units representing the fifteen weeks of his course. After distributing the general objectives, we began writing specific objectives for each. We got to week 3, at which point the professor decided he would complete this work for the remaining weeks of his course before we met again.

Session 3: Since our last meeting, over a month ago, the professor had sent me copies of his colleagues' syllabi, so we began with a discussion about the courses which were closest to his. We had independently come to the conclusion that there was no redundancy between the objectives in these various courses although there was just enough overlap between course objectives to ensure an acceptable level of pedagogical continuity. Reassured, we returned to working on his course.

With regard to his writing specific objectives for weeks 4 to 15, he told me that he had simply not had the time. Besides, he said, he had experienced 'technical difficulties' when he had started this work, not knowing how to proceed despite the models I had supplied. I came to the conclusion that, fundamentally, he didn't see the need to spend time drafting them because he asked me if it was worthwhile to students to have information provided to them in such detail (i.e. in the form of specific objectives). It seemed to me that he was obviously not ready to put in the time to do something that he didn't consider absolutely necessary. I tried explaining why creating a syllabus based on objectives, rather than on contents, was, from a design standpoint, essential. But my explanation didn't seem to influence him. Consequently, aware of the risk that he could decide, at any minute, to completely stop the design of his course, I decided to forego development temporarily. We spent the rest of our meeting discussing pedagogical strategies he might adopt in his course.

> *A linear model requiring systematic precision and rigour and structured with fixed design steps – despite its being very prominent in academic-based literature on ISD design theory – is a hard sell to professors with little time or patience. Their needs are of two types: immediate and specific. Even if I try to be linear and systematic in my application of the ISD model, I feel pressure to answer very specific needs (help in designing an exam, enriching a case study, designing a graphic representation for a PowerPoint, etc.) which, normally, should be addressed at a later step in the application of the ISD model. My attempts at prompting him to complete the steps of the model in sequence seem to diminish his will to carry on. (He often says to me that the model is very structured, doubtlessly meaning it's too structured). I thus find myself in a trade-off situation: I simply can't stand firm on principle without affecting the professor's motivation to continue, so I must deviate from applying the classical ISD model. This puts me in an intolerable position because, on the one hand, if I agree to betray the most fundamental principles of instructional design, doing so will likely result in a relatively inferior course. On the other hand, if I do not manage to respond to his perceived needs, he may abandon the design process. It is a classic dilemma. Ultimately, this situation has been created by the professor's lack of time to accomplish this task, given his numerous other responsibilities.*

Accepting to lose this battle while still hoping to win the war, I then moved on to the next step in the method, that of an analysing the teaching exercises he had used in the past as well as the contents they required. At this point, the professor started showing more interest in to the design process. The descriptions of his contents were essentially linked to a series of texts to be read by his students: articles, chapters or excerpts from books, sometimes his own notes, all of it comprising compulsory reading. In reference to his documentary search, he stated that he based his course on textbook cases which were fundamental to understanding the field, on commentary from experts as well as newly emerging case studies. His intent was to keep his materials up to date.

Returning to the general objectives now in each of the 15 units, we proceeded to distribute course content based on those objectives. As we went through his course materials, we analyzed the linkage between the various course contents and the objectives. I, playing the devil's advocate, asked him to explain his reasoning behind the choices he had made. He seemed amazed by this turn of events and he said, somewhat defensively, that this was the first time he had actually thought about it out loud, so to speak, being used to working alone with little feedback from his colleagues. He said that he found this was a difficult and sometimes annoying process. Yet he said that he also had the feeling that we were improving the internal logic of his course, indeed markedly so. Consequently, as we moved through the course, we kept making links between the general objectives and his contents because it allowed us to identify new links. As well, unforeseen links emerged which required our adding additional didactic resources. Finally, even if this exercise was time-consuming, it did greatly improve the overall structure of the course but did not modify its basic thrust. Given the fact that we spent much more time on this than anticipated, we now had to hurry because the professor had only three weeks more and about six hours each week to get everything done on the design of his course.

We continued to identify the didactic resources for the next weeks of his course, linking objectives to the course concepts and contents he intended to present. We also made significant changes to several units, based on the redundancy of some content elements and the absence of others, resulting in an improved clarification of intent on his part. Roughly speaking, the course remained intact although he now felt that it was better structured, researched and presented. He said he now felt more confident in presenting his course. By the end of this session, we had made it to Week 5 of his syllabus.

Session 4: We started this session by linking teaching resources to learner support activities. This required that we analyse his overall teaching strategy so as to identify the kinds of resources he needed and the activities required to support learners as they accessed the resources. Up until now, the professor had basically limited his analysis to identifying the reading material (resources) he expected his students to cover. I emphasised the need for supplementary learner support activities which would allow them to better utilize the resources he provided. After discussing the matter and understanding the distinction between didactic resources and learning activities, he said he felt "more informed, more enlightened."

Given the fact that the professor had earmarked a substantial number of readings for his course, we decided to develop learner support activities to help students better synthesize all of the information they were expected to manage.

> *As we proceed, he seems to understand the extent to which course design, in order to be effective, has to possess a learner-enabling characteristic and that it is not sufficient to simply provide students with resources; there also has to be learning activities that require supporting learning resources.*

Given the considerable amount of reading to be done in this course, we decided to go through the required material for each week systematically and to identify learner support activities for each unit. The result of this process was the development of reading comprehension exercises (RCEs) which we hoped would help students focus on the main concepts and summarize the highlights of each text.

> *The professor's initial difficulty in understanding the difference between the "teaching resources" concept as opposed to the "learner support activities" concept and the ensuing discussion prompts my thinking that applying the KISS principle (keep-it-simple-sweetheart) in such cases might not be a bad idea, since what may appear to an ID as an essential characteristic of good design could easily be interpreted by faculty as just nitpicking. So I'm starting to think that for design to succeed, at least in higher education, it has to be stripped down to its basics and only the essentials retained. Note to self: stop confusing faculty!*

As work on linking his content to learning activities progressed, we diverged somewhat and began discussing how he would conduct his weekly videoconference. He explained that he mainly used the "open discussion" method. To that end, he required that his students read the weekly-assigned case studies before coming to the weekly videoconference. We then discussed posting his materials online. At the time, he didn't have a website but he did want to develop one, seeing numerous advantages in doing so. For instance, he wanted to avoid the hassle of photocopying and also wanted to post a series of PowerPoint presentations he had done earlier. He did however mention his uneasiness with any form of programming which might be required, unless it were simply drag and drop.

The professor then began discussing expectations that several of his colleagues had, as well as numerous students, with regard to what constituted good teaching. He said a lot of his colleagues considered that the ultimate course, a real course, is a good lecture. He said most of them paid lip service to a need for in-class dialogue, seemingly resigned to the fact that most students preferred to be passive in class. This he felt was the worst possible situation and he went on to describe what I recognized as a socio-constructivist approach to learning. He described the role of the professor in engineering discussion, in keeping students on track and on subject, basing their comments on their readings. He said he tried to keep a balance between the wax and wane of discussions in class and to avoid intervening too much while also making sure none of them spoke too much. He also berated some of his colleagues who appeared to believe that they knew everything there was to know in their field and felt compelled to share it all with their students (i.e. telling them). He connected this traditional approach to the issue of control in the classroom.

Since our time was running out and I had wanted to make sure that he felt ready to begin his course, I asked him whether he had experienced any specific difficulties in the course, i.e., parts where students tended to get bogged down. He said his major problem was that he simply had too much information to cover. He added that, after the first time he gave this course, he had realized that it was necessary to cut back on the material but that he had no idea of how to do that. When I asked him why there was so much to cover, he said it had to do with the wide variety of required subjects that often defied easy categorization. But he said he did try to give priority to some elements and highlight certain cases. I asked him on what basis he ranked cases, he answered: "Usually on the basis of the more frequently-cited cases, but especially on the relevance of cases to current issues."

With regard to difficulties in his course, he showed me a series of transparency-based diagrams he had already used and planned to use again. We spent time redesigning them to improve their intelligibility.

As for posting resources on the Web, the technical team had produced a tutorial explaining how to upload material to the LMS. This tutorial was available online and delivered in asynchronous mode. Furthermore, the university retained the services of a student association to supply technical support services over the phone. The professor said that, given his time constraints, he would try to get a teaching assistant (TA) to upload his materials.

Session 5: Between sessions, the professor had produced a series of reading comprehension exercises (RCEs). He had taken a series of in-class quizzes and rewritten them as exercises. We then redesigned a number of questions so that they were more in tune with the general objective for each week. In certain cases, we had to write entirely new questions. While we did this work, I had the opportunity to identify the specific objectives he seemed to be aiming at and inserted them into the syllabus after he had signed off on them. Since our time together was nearly over, the professor told me he was ready to finish the work for the remaining weeks of the course, according to the model we had established.

Towards the end of this session, I sent the exercises we had completed for his course to a member of our technical team whose job it was to assist faculty in placing them on their website. The professor said that this parallel development of didactic materials and reading comprehension exercises (RCEs) went a long way in helping him redesign and ultimately improve his course.

Session 6: This session began with a discussion about student performance assessment. We had to take into account the emphasis he placed on the individual acquisition of knowledge and his doubts about teamwork, but we also recognized the need to motivate students to participate actively in this course. The professor decided to allocate 75 percent of his course points to individual performance, namely, 25 percent for the RCEs, 25 percent for a mid-quarter exam and 25 percent for the final exam. He then decided to attribute the remaining 25 percent to participation in team exercises to be completed in the online discussion forum between weekly sessions.

Since the time available to us was relatively short, we contented ourselves with identifying RCEs that would be marked (some were being used only for formative evaluation) and checking the level of congruency between the specific objectives and the questions. Having established a functional *modus operandi*, the professor once again said he was willing to complete this work between our sessions.

As we design his course and, more specifically, write his course objectives, we begin examining his mid-term and final exams to check the level of congruency between his objectives and exam items. This allows us to identify objectives which had apparently gotten lost in some of the units/ modules but, considering their weight in the exams, had to be identified in the syllabus. This kind of study of the correlation between exam items and course objectives constitutes a good example of reverse engineering in design, a useful technique in cases where it is difficult to identify the objectives a faculty member actually wishes to set or in cases where the professor is not inclined to invest much time in writing them.

One difficulty the professor experienced during this fine-tuning session was differentiating between specific objectives and exam items. I turned to Dick & Carey (2000) and to Morissette (1984) to explain the difference. I realize that a short workshop on writing objectives and exam items, delivered using educational software, would probably be quite useful to professors working autonomously. (NB. The most recent version of Dick & Carey came out in 2007.)

Session 7: Our last working session dealt with the issue of access to resources. We were faced with a decision: either allow learners to simply download the course materials posted on the site (case studies, texts, RCEs, etc.) or limit their access by allowing them viewing and printing privileges only when they were online. The professor considered this decision problematic because he was concerned that his copyright and intellectual property rights might be threatened. According to our support team, technically speaking, it was simpler to just allow students to download .pdf files, and especially .doc or .ppt files, so that they could study them later and/or complete them offline. This approach worried the professor because he was afraid his materials would become the prey of hackers and even sold online. Finally, after a discussion with the technical support team, we opted for a halfway solution: students would be able to access and download the course material but only in .pdf format. The professor was reassured that his material was somewhat protected, at least with regard to the average student, but this approach limited the level of interactivity that students could have with the resources. Our meeting with the technical team concluded my work on this course. The professor continued working for a time with a technical assistant to produce several digitally-configured documents that we had designed together.

Conclusion

At the end of this first case, I saw that the time this professor had been able to dedicate to the design of his course was very limited, usually no more than three hours of working together and three hours of work on his own per week. However, the classical ISD design model which was the basis for my prototype and which guided the design process over this six-week period required at least twice the time he had available. We had never completed any one step, whether it was the analysis of his course, the overall design of it or, for that matter, any of the others usual steps. We would begin an analysis, I would explain certain concepts using examples to support what I was saying and then I would have to move on to the following step. Since the professor's participation was more or less voluntary, I could in no wise pressure him into completing any agreed-upon task between working sessions. When I tried to inquire into progress being made (like his writing specific objectives), his answers tended to be elusive. Consequently, I was unable to ascertain what exactly he had completed in his course. I was often under the impression that the work had been postponed in the face of more urgent priorities. Another thing I noticed was that the professor had a fair degree of difficulty balancing the design/redesign of his course with his regular activities. He gave me the distinct impression that the time he dedicated to his course design work deprived him of research time.

Ex Post Facto Interview

On the student support activities dimension and more specifically about the role of dialogue in this process: Is dialogue important? "Yes, in my view, it is. It's what defines the educational experience...For instance, take what MIT has done; they've put their course contents on the Web. Now, that is not teaching...There is a difference between course materials and interaction, like quality dialogue. Learning is a process of common investigation based on the exchange of information and perspectives. Dialogue is an opportunity to question one's own understanding, to question that of others, to think in a critical and creative way but also to think in an empathic way. Passivity for the student is fatal."

On pedagogical issues: "My students receive a lot of information. I speak to them about issues, about ideas, about arguments and about conclusions...it is our frame of reference. I ask them to position themselves accordingly: what is their position with regard to each idea and issue? On what do they base their opinions, how do they come to a conclusion? How can this position influence them in their career? I want to move them in the direction of knowledge-building. I present them with different cases but what's important is how they react to a given situation. By seeing how real people act and react in various situations, they can better position themselves."

On the importance of eye contact: "It's very important, usually, but I can adapt. To listen to someone without seeing them is OK, so long as we can share documents."

On distance education: "It's somewhat advantageous for professors but especially interesting for students. But I'm ready to teach at a distance to increase my students' access to higher education."

On delivering the course by videoconference: he told me he had experienced "...a degree of apprehension at the beginning because of the novelty. I had no previous experience (with videoconferencing). There were technical glitches ...I was cut off, ...sound quality was unsatisfactory, the computer screen kept freezing, I couldn't move around the classroom like I'm used to doing but, as I get used to it, things should go better."

On comparing lecturing to Web-based courses: "If it's just for a presentation and if you can get the same thing on the Web, why go to class? Is it the same thing? Hmm, maybe to experience a feeling of belonging to a group? I wonder if that is so important...If we take the case of my graduate students for example, would they be ready to drop the 'learning community' experience? Yes, they have already done that with the videoconference courses."

On the use of technology in teaching: "I agree [with using technology] insofar as I can be guaranteed good quality exchange and dialogue. In that case, yes, OK. If we use technology, it has to work to support the work of professors."

(Note: this interview was conducted months after the above-described case study was completed).

Notes

1. See the Appendix 1 for a full description of the "Congruency Principle." The "Method" is a proprietary document which cannot be reproduced.

CASE STUDY 2
Beating the Clock

Case Characteristics

Table 4: Characteristics of the subject matter expert

Gender	Rank	Reason	Time	Availability	No. of sessions	K/ Design	K/ DE	GO/ SO
F	AST	0	1	1	6	1	2	2

Gender: female

Rank: AST = assistant

Reason: O = organisational

Time-to-delivery: 1 = course already begun or is about to begin

Availability: 1 = minimally available (1-15 hrs)

Number of sessions = 6

Knowledge of Design 1 = low level

Knowledge of DE: 2 = has never offered distance courses

General Obj. /Specific Obj.: 2 = GOs only

Case 2 is similar to Case 1, with three differences: the professor is a she, not a he; the course start date is one and a half months away, instead of four to six; and the number of working sessions ended at six.

This professor already had a course syllabus and had taught this course once before on campus. Considering the fact that she had approximately one and a half months before the course was to begin, the professor anticipated our not being able to meet very often. Consequently, we decided to get down to brass tacks. For my part, I felt it would be best to be non-directive and try to restrict my involvement to answering her questions.

> *Judging by these first two cases, it looks like I am in for ongoing "rapid design," a euphemism for not having enough time to do the job right. Under normal circumstances, a designer can expect six months to redesign a course, and even that is a short amount of time. Ideally, a year is not too long. To check my reasoning, I consult with several fellow designers at other dual-mode universities; they confirm that having at least two terms to design a course is not a luxury. So I'm thinking, if these cases are in any way representative of what's to come in this dual-mode university, my design prototype will likely have to continue to evolve and evolve quickly to adapt to what thus far seems to be "the way things are" (quoting the movie* Babe).

Session 1: This time, instead of asking the professor to go through the *congruency* and *method* presentations on her own, I sat with her for about half an hour, during which time I presented her the design approach I envisaged. She seemed relatively interested in my explanations about course planning, the steps I was proposing and the stages to be followed but, at the same time, I also felt anxiety on her part to get at designing her course.

I followed up by asking her if she had seen the presentations, which she had. She didn't have any specific questions about them. We began our work by conducting a global analysis of her course syllabus, positioning it inside the program of which it is a component. Like the professor in Case 1, she had not seen the syllabi of the other courses in the program and did not know what the objectives were for the other courses. She agreed to obtain copies of these syllabi, to ensure that her course objectives did not overlap with those of any of the other courses.

After further study of her course syllabus, I noted it was designed along the same lines as the model current among faculty in her department. It was basically a course summary presenting the usual elements found in a syllabus of this type: the course title, professor's coordinates, a general description of the course, its purpose, its general objectives, its contents (in the form of thematics), student performance assessment guidelines and, finally, a list of bibliographical references. The subjects to be studied were subdivided into book chapters or separate readings, but the syllabus provided no idea of how students would progress week-by-week through the course.

The very first task I proposed we undertake was to identify the subjects to be studied and the associated resources to be used in each week of the course. By removing the first class (during which the professor usually only has time to discuss the syllabus with students and, perhaps make some introductory remarks about the course), then reading week (spring or fall break) and finally exam week from the schedule, there remained only twelve weeks. We then allocated reading material for each of these twelve weeks, avoiding assigning students too much or too little in each. After doing a rough distribution of the readings, we revised her general objectives (which were grouped at the beginning of her syllabus) and distributed them throughout her syllabus, one or two per week.

Afterwards, the design process became rather random. She told me that her immediate concern was developing the initial learning activities/exercises she for her students. I proposed we start by developing team exercises (TEs). This type of exercise was new to her, so I took time to explain the importance of such activities from a socio-constructivist perspective and emphasized the necessity of creating the most relevant exercises possible in light of the objectives to be reached. We returned to her syllabus and, after breaking down the general objectives, we started identifying specific objectives (SOs) for the first two weeks of classes. We were then able to identify TEs that were directly linked to her SOs. Students would be required to accomplish the TEs in teams of four or five, depending on the numbers enrolled in her course. The TEs were designed to help her better supervise her students because, according to the scholarly literature (Colbeck, Campbell & Bjorklund, 2000; Laurillard, 1993; Millis & Cottell, 1998), teamwork and peer-to-peer coaching has been amply demonstrated to be particularly effective in enhancing learning, especially for retention and motivation, with the advantage of requiring little involvement or time investment on the part of faculty, other than an upfront description of exercise completion guidelines and a follow-up synthesis. The kinds of team exercises we developed were, for the most part, based on weekly readings, often consisting of open-ended questions for debate, the results of which would be shared in class, seminar-style.

She also wanted to discuss videoconferencing (V/C), with which she had little experience. These weekly virtual meetings were organized according to the same schedule as campus-based courses and lasted as long, i.e. three hours with a twenty-minute break at midpoint. Since this was the first time she was to deliver a distance education course, she asked me to explain the difference between on-campus teaching and teaching via videoconferencing: limitations, guidelines, tips, resources requiring development, etc., which I did.

In hindsight, I realize that I probably downplayed any real differences between in-class teaching and teaching via videoconferencing, likely in an unconscious (or semi-conscious) attempt to allay her fear of starting this course. There are, of course, differences, especially with regard to faculty mobility in class. Those who are used to moving about (writing on the board, interacting spontaneously with students) may feel a bit stymied by the limits of V/C, at least given the technical set-up we had at our disposal. Our set-up required the professor to move as little as possible so as to not interfere with audio and video quality, ideally using the document camera rather than the SmartBoard *(which seemed to serve no purpose whatsoever), all the while not forgetting to switch back to the headshot camera after using the document camera.*

Afterwards, at her request, we began to analyze the compulsory readings in her course. She had already chosen a textbook and other reading material (mostly short articles and case studies). This brought us to the work of developing reading comprehension exercises that students could be expected to complete after doing the readings. I realized that since the professor was used to teaching on-campus, she presented a lot of her guidelines and instructions verbally. Therefore, I suggested that she document everything she told her students in class, so as to add it to her learning exercises. We then developed the first reading comprehension exercise (RCE) of the course, which would serve as a model for elaborating subsequent exercises. Doing so brought us to the topic of objectives and how they might form the basis for "modularizing" her course, i.e. "chunking" it (Reigeluth, 1999).

We worked on identifying her expectations in the most precise way possible. For instance, she had a number of fundamental must-see elements (e.g., the scientific foundations of her discipline), which she intended to present to her students at the beginning of her course. The very act of identifying a specific number of elements seemed to help her stay within the available time each week of her course. We continued identifying her RCEs, and also other individual assignments that students were expected to do (and which were to be marked), such as oral presentations about theoretical approaches. Intuitively following an emerging, iterative design pattern brought us around, once again, to talking about team exercises, namely team presentations. Considering the fact that this professor neither knew exactly how many students would be enrolled in her course, nor where they would be enrolled (on the main campus or at a satellite campus), it was difficult to anticipate the size of the teams or even the types of teams, i.e. virtual or location-based, that would emerge. While waiting for this information, we discussed team exercises dealing with the simplification of some key concepts. In this regard, one of their assignments was to develop a conceptual map of an abstract concept, based on a model the professor would supply to serve as an advance organizer, *à la* Ausubel (1963). We discussed which guidelines should be provided to students to prevent their reproducing the model they were given, which they might do in the absence of clear instructions.

After completing that exercise, we once again returned to the readings chosen for her students (which represented her principal learning resource) and we began distributing them throughout her course. In this way, we positioned the readings to be done, week by week. At this point, the professor wanted to analyse the contents of the readings, to make sure that there was proper "concept chaining" (her term) and also to discuss the limits she wished to set for this course. After analyzing and adjusting the linkage between all concepts and the linkage between the concepts and the readings, we ended this long session by inserting into her syllabus bibliographical resources to clarify elements presented in the textbook and to offer alternative perspectives.

Bouncing around from one problem to the next makes me realize to what extent an ID must be flexible while accompanying faculty through the design process. The professor is naturally nervous as she approaches teaching her first course via videoconferencing and this nervousness translates into a muddled session during which we move haphazardly through various design stages. Flexibility appears to be necessary, for had I remained faithful to the usual design phases and advanced through each one systematically (finishing each stage before moving on to the next) she'd likely have abandoned the process by now and forged on ahead alone, doing as she saw fit. However, by attempting to answer her most urgent questions and by finding concrete solutions to her immediate and particularly vexing problems, I believe I managed to provide her with the kind of help she needs, albeit not the kind I had envisioned.

Session 2: The professor informed me that she wanted, during this session, to focus on assessing student performance by reviewing the various instruments of measure and evaluation that she had already developed for her course. Based on previous experience, she knew that she wanted her students to complete a quiz every three weeks, carry out a team project and write two exams, one at mid-term and the other at the end of term. Moreover, she wanted to encourage student participation in various course exercises, such as the online discussion forum and the videoconferencing-based weekly class. We also discussed allocating points for participation. We reviewed her existing assessment instruments, taking special care to rewrite her guidelines for students. Before ending our conversation on this subject, we also looked at her marking scheme and her clearly-identified assessment criteria.

On participation: in most cases, professors enjoy complete freedom in identifying the number of points that they wish to assign to student participation in their courses. According to available information (gleaned from discussions with faculty teaching in the Humanities), among the professors who assign points for participation (not all do), the total number of points usually varied between 10 to 15 percent of the final mark. However, I later learned that participation didn't seem to matter in some faculties (such as in the Physical Sciences), where it was only expected that students be successful in their exams.

We also discussed the pros and cons of paper versus electronic assignment submittal as well as how to manage the additional workload of supporting students working at a distance.

At this point, I begin thinking about the progress we have made during our working sessions. I realize that the professor has taken little notice of the design model I had proposed to her at the outset. Was she not interested in the model and in its different steps or does she simply not understand it? When I first spoke to her about steps, namely analysis and module-building, she seemed to understand these concepts, but as for the others, teaching strategies and learner support, they appear to be vague to her. She does not seem capable of distinguishing between, on the one hand, designing her teaching resources and, on the other, designing learner support activities. I decided to try a new tack.

I then spoke to her about the importance of identifying all the elements which were to be presented to her students during a given week, one week a time. We thus returned to the elements we had created up until then: the objectives, the contents (or materials) and the teaching and learner support exercises and resources. It was at this point that, in order to put everything together, I understood that we should develop a grid to help us visualize all of these elements.

> *At this point, I'm starting to imagine a different course syllabus, one that would facilitate visualizing the whole course at one glance. Instead of the traditional syllabus model used in most universities (for instance, see various syllabi at the* University of Texas World Lecture Hall: http://web.austin.utexas.edu/wlh/*) and which is, for the most part, essentially characterized by its verticality—the composite elements being aligned from top to bottom—I could now see the necessity of aligning these elements on a horizontal plane so that the students could see, in a clear and precise way, what was expected of them (objectives), what they had to work with (content) and when they would be doing it (exercises).*

Session 3: The professor had obtained the syllabi for the other courses in the program, so we began their analysis and found that there was no major overlap between her objectives and those of these other courses. Having satisfied our curiosity, we turned our attention back to the study of her syllabus which, in light of the above reflection, was a decidedly vertical course syllabus.

During this session, we returned to the question of objectives, namely the general objectives for her course. The initial distribution of her general objectives had not been made on a weekly basis but rather by dividing the course roughly into four parts (which she called units). We began re-dividing her course up into weekly components so as to make it easier for students to understand what they were to do and when they were to do it. She agreed and so we redistributed her general objectives at the rate of at least one per week.

As in the previous case, the professor had never had the time or taken the time to finish writing her objectives because her department did not require faculty to define specific objectives in their syllabus. Consequently, I only had a rough idea of her expectations *vis-à-vis* her students, as I believe she did. To remedy this, we began identifying specific objectives for each general objective. Like the professor in the previous case, she at first had difficulty writing her objectives, but we worked at it until we had completed the first four weeks of the course. At that point, she said (rather dismissively) that she would use the same model to finish writing the objectives for the remaining weeks (Weeks 5 to 14) but I had my doubts. Again, my explanations of the necessity of creating a course syllabus based on objectives rather than on content did not hit home. Consequently, given this manifest lack of interest on the part of the professor for writing objectives, I decided to limit any further intervention on my part to a revision of her general objectives.

Over the years that I've worked with faculty, one thing I frequently notice is, when faculty write objectives, they tend to do so from their own point of view, rather than from the point of view of learners; that is, they tend to write about their teaching objectives rather than students' learning objectives. Furthermore, the specific objectives tend to be either too general (non-operational and virtually immeasurable) or too specific (a series of tasks to be carried out, more like exam items than objectives). Not for the last time in these case studies, confusion about objectives versus exam items, tasks, steps, and so on resurfaced.

Again, I was confronted with a professor's manifest indifference to writing objectives. Either she did not see the necessity of doing so, or the urgency, or both. She mentioned her concern that clearly defining objectives "reveals too much" to students, in turn making exams and tests "too easy." Like the professor in Case 1, she did not see any value in "laying everything out for them" [the students].

In my view, this exemplifies how unimportant faculty consider writing objectives as compared to writing course content. It is at the cost of sacrificing objectives that courses are developed. Moreover, in the original syllabi, I noticed that the main part of virtually every one deals with contents, sometimes divided into sub-sections, units or modules. These professors are very aware of "elements" they want to "cover" (a favourite verb among faculty) with their students as well as the order in which they want to present them, but when I ask them questions about what the point is (i.e. the objective) of covering this content, they tend to be evasive.

This obvious lack of interest on the part of faculty for objectives-writing (and the recurring pattern of resistance to doing so) is starting to make me question the usefulness of objectives higher education. Maybe faculty have a point. It is a fact that instructional design as a field of practice, and subsequently of research, didn't start in universities, but in the military and then in industry, where it is of the utmost importance to train personnel for competency, skills mastery and other observable activities. It is also important in large organizations that large numbers of individuals receive the same training and be brought to the same competency threshold. Maybe that was the problem? Faculty see themselves as being responsible for arousing intellectual curiosity in their students, of developing minds and sharpening intellects, but they definitely do not see themselves as mere "trainers," aiming to reach objectives. So, how applicable is instructional design to higher education? Now there's something to think about...

Afterwards, we returned to examining linkage between course contents from one week to the next as well as their sub-division into exercises. This activity seemed to hold more interest for the professor. Our analysis of her course contents revealed a certain level of redundancy in the didactic resources she provided to students. We saw some overlap in the proposed readings and recognized that students did not need to read 40 to 50 pages of text to be able to attain the weekly general objective. Thus, we spent some time analyzing her intended course content as well as its format. As mentioned, her course content was mainly comprised texts to be read, sometimes articles, sometimes book chapters or excerpts from books, sometimes the professor's course notes. We then proceeded to distribute these contents throughout the course according to the already-identified general objectives, in conformity with proper ISD practice although running counter to a well-established faculty practice of first identifying the contents and then identifying the objectives. As we made our way through her content, we analyzed linkage between elements and, always playing the devil's advocate, I asked her questions about her reasoning behind various choices of elements and why certain elements were linked. She told me that this was the first time she had ever gone through this process with anyone else, being used to working without feedback from anyone, even colleagues. Although she found it was a "difficult and sometimes annoying process," she had the feeling that we were "greatly improving the internal logic" of her course. As a result of noticing a lack of resources in some cases, she had to identify other potential sources of content in order to complete her course. Nevertheless, she had already identified about 80 percent of the documentary resources she would be using.

Finally, in spite of the fact that we could have spent many more hours on it, we had to hurry because the professor only had about six hours a week to spend in completing her course. So, by the time this long (and winding) working session drew to a close, we had managed to get to Week 5 of her syllabus.

Session 3: This week, we decided to complete the process of identifying the didactic resources for the remaining weeks of her course. This work went well. Once again, we closely examined her concept-chaining and made some minor changes. Roughly speaking, the course remained intact.

Discussion then ensued on delivering her didactic resources. These were slated to be available on the course website, either as documents which could be opened and modified online or downloaded and modified and then resaved offline. The question of access to these resources was, in the eyes of this professor, of the highest importance. We were facing what she considered a major decision: either to allow learners to simply download the didactic resources or to limit access by only allowing them to be viewed as non-modifiable, on-screen resources while students were online. The professor perceived this decision to be problematic from the point of view of copyright law and intellectual property. According to our support team, technically speaking, it was simpler to allow students to download what usually amounted to .doc, .ppt or .pdf files, so that they could study them, complete the assignments, and then post them for marking. The professor was afraid students might keep copies on their hard drives and sell them online. As a consequence, she preferred severe limits on student access to her documents.

In retrospect, her decision to limit access to her documents, taken during discussions with the support team, appears to have been a means for the team to reassure her, even lull her into a false sense of security. With regard to the average student, this solution did seem to offer the professor a better level of security for her intellectual property. But, as we all know, if there is sufficient motivation, any student can reproduce and redistribute whatever appears on their screens. The down side to her decision was the limit on students' interactivity with the didactic resources, unless the support team were to invest a considerable number of hours in producing each resource in a protected format. As it turned out, the problem of IP would to continue to haunt us throughout the entire case study process.

Session 4: We now moved on to the analysis of a student support strategy which would complete the professor's teaching strategy. Indeed, considering the considerable amount of reading to be done by students in this course, we decided to supply learners with two types of exercises to improve content-learner dialogue.

Type 1: individual exercises
Type 2: team exercises

Type 1 exercises aimed at producing a first level of understanding of the texts being read, i.e. terminology acquisition, at both the abstract and theoretical levels and at the level of what I termed "learner cognitive positioning" (inspired by Skehan, 1998), meaning the student would read texts and answer questions which required his or her taking a position on issues raised. Type 2 exercises were intended to allow the learners to compare their answers from the Type 1 exercises with their teammates and, bearing in mind a socio-constructivist approach to learning (Sullivan-Palincsar, 1998), to negotiate the answers obtained. This exercise was intended to allow learners to reconcile their viewpoints with those of their co-learners.

Given the fact that this course was going to be delivered at a distance with about thirty students distributed over five sites, it was necessary to envisage appropriate means of follow-up and supervision. Because an existing agreement had established that this course would be delivered live by videoconferencing at the rate of three hours a week, with learners congregating at any one of five available videoconferencing sites, this meant the principal means of providing learners with feedback on their processing of the course didactic materials would be during this synchronous event. In addition, we established that the main means of asynchronous feedback would be via email and an online discussion forum because all of the learners had access to university-provided email accounts as well as to the course website.

I am reminded that I need some sort of tool with which I can better guide professors through the design model, such as a list of tasks they would carry out or, better still, a form they could complete. Consequently, I start developing a course syllabus template in the form of a synthesis grid, which could give form to the syllabus-development process. Based on my earlier reflection about vertically- as opposed to horizontally-designed course syllabi, I'm thinking that this synthesis grid (see Table 5) should be structured differently than the traditional/classical course syllabus in that it should have two dimensions: one vertical and one horizontal. The course would not be divided into modules or units but, for simplicity's sake, would be directly linked to the available time for each class period. As is the case for most three-credit college or university courses, total seat time is usually 45 hours, spread over 15 weeks. Hence, the grid would be divided into temporal units corresponding to each of these weekly course blocks. Weekly progress would be charted along the vertical axis line and the various course components (objectives, subjects/content and exercises) would be displayed along the horizontal axis to create a continuous link between every component. The connection between the design model and its representation as a functional synthesis grid seems natural. Having already decided to abandon too rigorous an insistence on the ISD model, I feel the new grid may indeed assist faculty in their course planning. I intend to implement this grid during the next working sessions, to see if I can get course design to finally take off.

I've now fully grasped that distinguishing between teaching, learner support and evaluation activities is more of a theoretical and academic interest rather than a universal and practical interest for faculty. To simplify matters, I could simply help them develop an exercise in which there was a teaching component (a resource), a student support component (like a series of closed- or open-ended questions) and an evaluation component (limits, conditions and performance criteria). Also, professors could decide whether an exercise would "count" in students' final assessments or not.

Thinking about assessment makes me wonder how well we are using "class time." In a traditional course, a professor spends approximately three hours a week presenting his or her content to students and then he or she requires them to spend approximately six hours outside class studying (completing course individual or team activities). In our case, courses are delivered via weekly videoconferences so the same number of hours of seat time is usually maintained. *The remaining six hours of activities also fall into the same pattern as on-campus courses but, in general, increased use of electronic media is becoming the norm:*

- *compulsory reading that the professor provides, either as a hard copy or increasingly, electronically, to students;*
- *class notes and guidelines are increasingly posted online on a professor's website;*
- *teaching resources (.ppt presentations with attached audio tracks, 2D or 3D animations, .pdf-formatted texts, audio or video-based documents to be studied by students before class, etc.);*
- *individual or team exercises based on course readings but, increasingly, on websites to be researched, etc.;*
- *increasing interest on the part of faculty not only to allow students to exchange ideas online in the discussion forum and via email, but also their interest in participating in such exchanges.*

These examples of "blended learning" whereby classroom activities spill over into cyberspace appear to be enriching the didactic relationship between faculty and students but also, seem to be increasing faculty workload. How much enrichment can faculty support?

Table 5 : The synthesis grid model

	Design phases					
Week	1	2	3	4	5	6
	Analysis	Module-Building	Teaching Activities Development	Learner Support Activities Development	Evaluation Instruments Development	Items for Ongoing Improvement
X						

This fourth meeting concluded work on Case 2. It had been a short yet highly productive course design project and it had given me new insight to carry on. What had become an incredibly frustrating experience suddenly got a lot easier... and interesting. The synthesis grid held the hope of providing faculty with a new tool which might speed up their course design and speed seemed to be of the essence, given the small amount of time I'd been given to work with.

Ex Post Facto Interview

On the instructional design process: "This design process allows for a high level of student autonomy, and because of this I'm finding it hard… I have to be rigorous in my planning of exercises and activities and in my guidelines…I'm always wondering: "Is it enough?" With distance courses, everything has to be planned, when possible; we can't just let things happen randomly or spontaneously."

On team activities: "I used to get students to work together as teams in class. Now, I get them to work together before class. So I feel that there is less contact (between me and my students); it is more distant…I have more difficulty checking on what they are doing. What's more is that, besides the distance students in the multimedia rooms, I also have students on-site in my classroom. When I pay attention to the distance students, those on-site feel left out…if the technology allowed me to do what I want to do, that would be great…like getting good quality audio."[…] "They always have an activity to do before coming to class, like an individual or team assignment. Should they have trouble with one or the other, I go over them in class, during the videoconference."

On the usual activities sequence (individual, teams and plenary session activities): "This is the 1st time I've done things like that. Did things work out? Yes and no. Yes, they [my students] appreciated the structure [of the course]. And no, they said they had too much work. I realized that I had to opt for either an individual activity or a team activity but not both in the same week. To worsen matters, it was a spring term course so everything was accelerated. I'll never do that again…there just wasn't enough time."

On weekly readings: "My students did their readings because they had assignments linked to the reading to hand in which I corrected, but not all the time. There was just too much had to correct every week, plus it was a crash course! So I did random checks, say 4 out of 12…that was the carrot I had to work with! Then I gave them points for participation, for simply handing in their assignments. I asked them to complete the assignments and to hand them in, but there were no points for right answers…it just wasn't possible."

On videoconferencing and the plenary session: "I always began by reviewing the assignments, questions they couldn't answer... I asked them to hand in their assignments in advance so that I'd have time to go over them but I had to do that in a hurry. Then, in class, I used the Socratic method of questioning. But, at a distance, there was this gap which was annoying, even "hellish." I'd ask a question... silence... then I'd ask it again ...while they had begun answering it. The next part of the course dealt with their presentations on the weekly course content. I usually asked them to draw me a diagram which represented the main concepts from the weekly readings and to organize everything in a visual representation, to show me that they had understood the material."

On teamwork: I had divided them into groups of three, triads."

On course designing and professorial workload: "Yes, absolutely, a distance course takes more time to plan but I had a course release to do this."

On technology: "I was having computer problems at the time...I wasn't receiving my e-mail. I didn't use the LMS e-mail because I found it confusing. But I'll likely have to start using it to separate my email because students send me their assignments directly every week... their presentations, assignments."

On using Web resources in class: "I identified a few sites but some disappear and it's frustrating. But I use it [the Web] more and more. There is obviously the language problem but I try to find French-language resources. (How do I use Web for educational purposes?) That depends on the site. I ask my students to search for precise information, to investigate these sites and then report of what they've found. I believe experiential learning is very important. I ask them questions open-ended questions like 'According to you'... 'in your opinion'...I ask them to make the link between their own personal experience (what they observe) and what the experts say."

On the students [enrolled in this course]: "It was a diverse group. They were from several fields but that was not a problem in itself. I am used to working in multiple areas at the same time. In such cases, I work more on a 'general' level, trying to provide all with relevant examples."

On using information and communication technology: "Yes, I use it technology] a lot in my teaching but also in my research. Like with Australia! We have only technology to bring us together. They are mostly asynchronous exchanges for the moment but, if possible, I'd like to move on to synchronous exchanges. Now that I have a new computer, I'm increasingly using technology. Also because of the new multimedia room, I avoid using chalk. I prefer to go directly to sites online and then maybe show a video, etc. We analyze sites in class and we criticize them. Then I show PowerPoint slides every week. I find Internet sites that can help some of my students who have difficulties, such as problems with language. They are supplementary resources for my course."

On course planning: "I get back the time [invested]. Certainly. My students have quite a bit of work to do outside class."

On using the forum: "I think of using it but I haven't yet got around to it."

On assessment: "I am not in the habit of thinking in dichotomous terms of individual evaluation versus team evaluation but I suppose that my assessment is essentially 100 percent individual because each student has to meet the course requirements. Then, assessment of teamwork is problematic because some students do not work. I use a self-evaluation grid plus a team evaluation instrument for which each student is asked to assess what he or she has done as well as his or her peers. But students are never going to 'squeal' on their peers...I have to admit it is a pain to manage, personally. So, since this way of assessing students is such a pain...I really don't know how to manage teamwork... and online to boot! It is more complicated. I believe teamwork is rich, especially in teams of three or four students, no bigger than that. Usually triads, not dyads, except for in-class for random assignments. I now try to get them to do their teamwork outside of class. But I have to admit I do have trouble managing teamwork at a distance."

On faculty's role in the future: "I have always spent a lot of time planning my teaching. I now think that with the new technology, I am going to be able to start offering my courses partly in real-time and partly in differed mode, but never again using videoconference. I would also like to participate more actively in the online forum. I want to get involved, to guide my students, to answer questions, to deepen their reflection. I can start teaching directly from my office. I do not think that the didactic relationship will be as rich (as our relationship in class) but it's possible."

On using the telephone to support learners: "On the telephone, we can't establish a real didactic relationship, not as much as in class. The non verbal is too important. Maybe the non verbal is 80 percent of the message. To see one another is important, that is if we want to avoid a 'pedagogy of just getting the answer right'...especially so in my particular field where the need for good communication is stronger than in other fields. I need to see my students...their faces. But I am able to adapt, I'm flexible."

CASE STUDY 3
EXPERIENCING A EUREKA! MOMENT

Case Characteristics

Table 6: Characteristics of the subject matter expert

Gender	Rank	Reason	Time	Availability	No. of sessions	K/ Design	K/ DE	GO/ SO
F	AST	0	2	1	7	1	1	3

Gender: female

Rank: AST = assistant

Reason: 0 = organisational

Time-to-delivery: 2 = beginning in between 2 to 4 months

Availability: 1 = minimally available (1-15 hrs)

Number of sessions = 7

Knowledge of Design 1 = low level

Knowledge of DE: 1 = has never offered distance courses

General Obj. /Specific Obj.: 3 = GOs + a limited number of SOs

Case 3 was not a lot different from Case 2. We had just a little more time to design this professor's course. However, this faculty member appeared to be just a bit less knowledgeable about instructional design and distance education than the previous one. Before our first meeting, I had asked the professor, as usual, to send me a copy of her current syllabus and I also invited her to go to my website to view both presentations on the congruency principle and the design model we'd be using. To save time, I obtained copies of the other course syllabi in her program from the Dean's office.

Session 1: This professor had never before seen the other syllabi comprising the program in which she taught. Being a relatively new member of the faculty, she had not taken part in the development of the program. As we looked at these syllabi together, we noticed that the objectives pursued, where they were explicit (certain courses contained only a few general objectives), aimed generally at the development of different competencies than those at which she was aiming at in her course. However, considering the wide variety of models used to design these syllabi and the variable level of detail in their presentation, I realized that the degree of certainty as to potential overlap of the objectives pursued in these courses was necessarily rather low.

We continued on, carefully examining her course syllabus. As in the other cases, I noticed that her plan had been designed according to the usual university model, with the main course components listed one after the other, all in a vertical pattern. Again, I noticed a general lack of congruency between the various parts of the syllabus and saw how arranging them on a grid would allow for a closer degree of correspondence between the objectives, the course contents, the individual and team exercises and, finally, the assessment instruments. I therefore presented the synthesis grid that I had just built for Case 2. She said she was interested in using it to convert her current syllabus but that she more immediate concerns which prevented her from doing so. We decided to discuss them first.

As she talks, my mind is elsewhere. The synthesis grid I had devised to support work in Case 2 could be reorganized to take into account further requirements which professors have vis-à-vis their students. In the synthesis grid, I had posited that the main functions of faculty, as per congruency (Power, 1996; see Appendix 1), were central in course planning. I am now realizing more and more that I have simply been perpetuating a faculty-centered course design perspective, whereas constructivist literature in instructional design (such as Jonassen, Peck & Wilson, 1999; Wilson, 1996) emphasizes the necessity of learner-centered course planning. I'm feeling that my haranguing faculty on the usefulness of writing objectives is a hen who has finally come home to roost in that I myself now have to apply the same logic to the way I approach course design.

As a result, I decide I can keep the grid idea but I have to completely re-conceptualize the synthesis grid (I never did like that name!) components. So I mentally remove the overly complicated Teaching Activities Development, Learner Support Activities Development *and* Evaluation Instruments Development *as well as the* Items for Ongoing Improvement *categories (see Table 5) and I replace them, in my mind, with three columns:* individual activities, team activities *and* plenary session activities. *Any instructional activity has to be done either alone or with others, hence the first two activities, and since we are currently using videoconferencing as the main means of course delivery, planning has to be done for the time spent in class, hence the* plenary session *column. Each activity will require clearly-presented guidelines and identification of available resources, criteria to be met and points to be allocated.*

Having done so, I see that this is probably as close as I'm ever going to get to a Eureka! *moment. It doesn't look like a breakthrough but it does have that feel. What I'm thinking is that, for once, students will have a grid in which everything of interest is there for them to see, at a glance. Moreover, each and every component in logically linked. This, in turn, leads me to think that perhaps a solution has been found to the perennial problem of the vertical course syllabus model in the sense that, in almost every course syllabus I have ever seen, objectives (if there are any) are found in a nice, tidy list somewhere towards the top of the syllabus but there they stay, unconnected to either course content or course assessment instruments. By linking all of these components on the horizontal plane, faculty can plan their course according to their intentions (objectives), linking these to the resources (readings) they put at their students disposal. Again, linking the resources to the actual activities they expect student do undertake, either individually or as part of a team, allows students to quickly understand what is expected of them, as well as when and how. In a matter of minutes, I feel I have arrived at something that will greatly change the focus of my course design pattern for some time to come.*

Coming back to reality, I hear the professor telling me about her immediate concerns, to which I now turn my full attention.

Her major problem concerned course delivery, i.e. the planned weekly videoconferences. She was worried about how to conduct these sessions, about the difference between teaching in-class and at a distance and she wondered if her pedagogy was going to suffer as a result of it. I explained to her that there were no fundamental differences between the two modes of course delivery because videoconferencing was really just the technological extension of what she was already doing in class. That said, I decided I should nuance my answer somewhat, so I added that there was, of course, the "distance factor"—transactional distance (Moore, 1993) does exist—and that the use of media in distance education can indeed affect pedagogy. However, the actual impact of such could vary from one professor to the next and from one class to the next. As this was her first time teaching via videoconferencing, she was naturally preoccupied with the technological dimension. I recommended that she get in touch immediately with the Continuing Education technical service so that she could get some practice using the V/C equipment, so as to feel more comfortable with it before beginning to teach in this environment.

We returned to her syllabus and I immediately went back into reflective mode on the synthesis grid idea.

My mind returns to the grid and the newly-emerged categories. I see that I have probably come to re-conceptualize the grid because of the severe constraints under which I have been working with faculty since Case 1. Lacking time, faculty availability, technical support, and so on, I have been frantically been searching for a solution, a short-cut in effect, something that would allow me to focus on design essentials, nothing more. I see that learning activities are the key...which brings to mind what Janovy (2003) said in Lessons from Cedar Point: *"course design consists primarily of the activities you ask your students to perform" (p. 67). That was it. The penny had dropped. So I get out some paper and redesign the grid on the spot (see Table 7).*

Table 7: Version 2 of the synthesis grid

Week	Objectives	Content or Themes	Individual Activities	Team Activities	Plenary Session Activities

Using this new grid, we started assessing the work required to convert her current plan into a new one. Because this course had a strong theoretical component, its primary didactic resource was readings from various sources. She had already distributed these texts throughout the course but there was no weekly division. As I explained this new grid to her, I also explained the usefulness of dividing her course into weeks of study (rather than units of study), to give her students a better idea of what was expected from them and when.

There is no universal standard for the length of any given course and many possible variations—a "regular" course can last from 12 to 15 weeks but, during the summer, it necessarily has a shortened schedule. This variance creates a supplementary difficulty when designing an online, media-rich course because they require a fixed schedule considering the planning required because of the use of technology and also the quantity of work demanded (generally greater than in "regular" courses). For the moment, because we are using V/C to replace on-campus classes, increased workload is not yet a problem, but I can see it looming. The administration is trying to get more and more faculty to develop full online courses to be delivered asynchronously to self-pacing students.

After a temporary weekly distribution of her texts for the term, we started discussing learning activities. I told her about the *individual activities* and *team activities* concepts and I explained the usefulness of writing such for each week of class. She already had a number of exercises and assignments in her original syllabus. We therefore began reconstructing her syllabus using the new grid, switching over exercises and assignments, identifying which would best be completed individually and which as a team. This session ended with our having partially completed the grid.

Session 2: At the very beginning of this session, the professor asked me to explain what modes of assessment I thought was best in her newly-redesigned course. By mode of assessment she meant:

- The *way* in which the assessment will be conducted, such as in either real-time (or synchronous) mode or in deferred (or asynchronous) mode, and
- The *formula* according to which assessment will be conducted, i.e. the form of the different assessment instruments.

To begin, she explained how she assessed students when her course is offered on campus. She usually gives a mid-term, development question-based exam, sometimes called a *complex production* (Scallon, 1993) in class. She also had a final, take-home exam. Moreover, she added oral presentations to the assessment mix, done by two-person teams. I explained that it was possible to evaluate her recently-enrolled distance education students using the same assessment instruments she used on campus, with only a few minor modifications.

Mid-term: students who attend her course at a distance could write her usual mid-term exam either in a room with a supervisor (by proxy, an established practice at this university), or via videoconferencing, where the professor herself would supervise, keeping a watchful eye on her remote classroom.

Final: instead of handing in a hard copy of their final exam, students could simply send her it by email, as an attachment. There are student-accessible computer laboratories on all three satellite campuses. Furthermore, everywhere in the province, students have access to community-based, Internet access centres (such as at libraries, etc.);

Oral presentations: she could continue to mark oral presentations presented by teams via videoconferencing.

In addition to the real-time assessment methods of videoconferencing and email, I told her about the university's new automated or semi-automated evaluation tools in the new Learning Management System (LMS). These tools, implemented in asynchronous mode, allowed teaching personnel (professors, sessionals or adjunct faculty) to post their contents in a password-protected environment. They required about 12 hours of training to learn how to use. I also spoke to her about automated evaluation tools in synchronous mode that the team and I had been investigating, various software and online systems that allow for real-time, two-way dialogue with full sharing-screen, etc. She said she was interested in discovering how useful these types of course delivery systems would be for her as soon as she has more time.

We continued with a discussion of the objectives and content of the weekly plenary sessions. Instead of asking her students to do readings and activities before class, she intended to conduct a weekly, open-style lecture on a given theme with a continuous and spontaneous flow of questions and answers. Then she would ask her students to complete a team exercise followed by an individual exercise, to be completed after class. The activities sequence she envisaged seemed, at first, to be the opposite of the approach practiced by most of the other professors I had encountered to date in that they required their students to prepare before coming to class. I figured I had to ask her whether or not she provided feedback to her students on work accomplished after class. She answered in the affirmative, indicating that that was the first thing she did every week. Consequently, to accommodate what she felt was "her pedagogy," we made the required changes in the columns of the synthesis grid (see Table 8). In actual fact, what was accomplished after class was, of course, done before the next class so we were talking about the same thing.

Table 8: Version 2B of the synthesis grid

Week	Objectives	Content or Themes	Plenary Session Activities	Team Activities	Individual Activities

Using a reworked version of the synthesis grid, we began transferring components from her old syllabus to her new one, dividing the course contents into weeks of activities. Since she had not identified objectives for every week, we also identified a general objective and several specific objectives for each one. The professor didn't seem to be enthralled by this work but she did agree to do it for the first three weeks of her course.

Once again, that the designer is in a vulnerable position while undertaking this work as long as faculty question the very foundations of instructional design. If designers have to justify their methodology every time they start designing a course, the work will not advance very quickly. There seems be a fundamental lack of confidence in the process of designing a course among faculty who doubt the usefulness of the exercise. How does a designer establish a climate of confidence? How can one persuade professors that instructional design is a domain of inquiry which is just as serious as their own fields? Decades of research have clearly demonstrated the relevance and the importance of a systematic method for designing instruction, the foundations of instructional design, which include identifying learning objectives. The lack of recognition of the instructional design profession by faculty members seriously delays the design of their course. Why can't they trust the ISD process? Is the field so little known and respected that instructional designers and researchers have to constantly justify themselves when working with other disciplines?

On the other hand, as mentioned earlier, Reiser (2001), made a point of saying that ISD has had little impact on higher education. It does ring true (from what I've seen)...for instance, although ISD is taught at university, it is rarely applied there...so why is that? Is there something about ISD that makes it incompatible with higher learning? Is it too basic a methodology – a process emerging primarily to respond to military and industrial exigencies in order to meet baseline training requirements – so, is it too basic to encompass the complexity of training highly qualified personnel (i.e. at the university level)?

Our conversation now returned to the issue of objectives with regard to assessment activities. We discussed two types of assessment, formative and summative. The professor said she was confused because, although she wanted to ensure proper supervision of her students, she did not want to spend all of her time correcting their work. We discussed finding a happy medium and developing instruments that could either be manually or automatically corrected. Basically, this gave me another chance to "sell" the need for objectives-writing because assessment items could only be developed for written objectives. "What other basis could there be for assessment?" I asked her. Given our limited selection of objectives, we managed to distinguish between what was most important to her in terms of learning outcomes and what was secondary. Finally, she told me that she wanted each of her students to process each of the case studies presented to them in the hope that they would be able to apply that knowledge in their work. So we returned to the objectives we had set for the first three weeks to begin work on developing the rest (GOs and some SOs) for subsequent weeks. After making some headway, we reviewed her learning activities in order to reflect the weight (in terms of points) attributed to each case study.

Session 3: We continued our work on student assessment. We had not yet defined what shape team activity assessments were going to take. The professor said she was against the principle of assessing teamwork because, in her experience, team members never provided the same level of effort in completing tasks. She preferred to encourage personal initiative rather than offering a "free ride to slackers." On the other hand, I emphasized that teamwork was in itself an excellent means of promoting certain types of learning, whether it was marked or not. I mentioned several constructivist-inspired studies (i.e. work by Bruner and Jonassen[1]) which shed light on the importance of negotiating meaning among learners which, in turn, facilitates knowledge accommodation and assimilation (Piaget, 1972). Without dialogue, without one's ideas confronting those of others, experience would be lessened.

We concluded by deciding to integrate teamwork as a preliminary requirement to individual work. It would be strongly suggested that students work in teams of two before completing individual activities. Oral presentations would henceforth be individual but that did not exclude preparation being conducted in teams. Because the professor felt she was unable to supervise the full participation of all students during their teamwork, she decided to assess them individually. She added that she aimed at monitoring individual student progress because, once out in the workforce, they would normally be called upon to work without the support of others, making decisions on their own and then assuming the consequences. For these reasons, she considered that her approach was justified.

Afterwards, we got into the details about the kind of professional tasks her students would have to carry out once they had graduated, to make sure that the different parts of her course effectively addressed the skill requirements. She explained that students, once in the field, would mostly be in "reaction mode," i.e. problem-solving. Hence, they would have to develop a strong capacity for resourcefulness. This exchange prompted me to speak to her about the heuristic approach based on algorithmic thinking. She didn't seem to understand just what that involved but she did demonstrate immediate resistance to the idea. "No, we don't do that," followed by "ahh, what is it exactly?" So I summarized some of the research in this field, e.g., Landa (1974) and applications of it by Zemke (1982). I explained how the approach was used in many fields, such as nursing, engineering, and computer science. Because her students would have to solve problems on an ongoing basis, the algorithmic approach might very well help them better understand the mental processes involved and which are activated when encountering a new problem. By first articulating their thoughts on to a given problem and then attempting to represent it visually in algorithmic format, they might experience improved levels of problem identification and problem-solving strategy sharing. We continued discussing this approach and, as we did, I started sketching out various schematics using simple cases to demonstrate how an algorithm constitutes a form of cognitive mapping (another concept I had to explain on-the-fly).

The example which seems to tilt the balance in favour of her using this approach is the one that I often use, that of an automobile mechanic who is training to become an automobile mechanics teacher. Having numerous years of experience as a mechanic, he is skilled in diagnosing problems and solving them. On the other hand, what he needs to develop is the skill of putting his diagnostic skills into words according to a logical sequence, thereby leveraging his honed skills of deduction and induction. For example, imagine the mechanic is faced with an engine problem. Now, according to the experts, most engine problems result from faulty electrical or mechanical components or a lack of fuel or air. The mechanic starts up the car and he immediately discovers a mechanical-sounding noise emanating from the starter. When hearing this, he immediately hypothesizes an electrical problem, thereby excluding a gas- or air-related problem. He knows, almost at once, that this is likely an electrical problem because of the sound the starter has made, it being an electrically-powered mechanical device connected to the battery. This simple example demonstrates that the mechanic, when confronted with a problem, has several hypothetical scenarios in mind, any one of which may turn out to be the problem, until he can exclude them one by one by testing. He is obviously going to lean towards one heuristic track rather than any other based on his intuitive, experience-based assessment of probable cause. It is this type of heuristics which he has to learn to put into words, ideally to model, and to present and represent to his students. This is the very foundation of competency and his ability to present it to students constitutes the quality of his mental models which, in turn, he may use to enable students to forge their own.

The more we spoke about this approach, the more the professor became interested in it as an instructional strategy. She recognized that she had actually used algorithms in her teaching (without knowing, before this discussion, what they were called) which helped her students understand the mental progresses they would have to implement in solving the problems they would likely encounter. We schematized examples from her field on-the-spot. In visualizing the various ramifications inherent in her algorithms, she said she was convinced of the interest in developing her students' competency in applying this skill during her course.

Session 4: As time was getting short, the professor wanted us to focus on a number of decisions she had to make for her course. For example, she asked me what needed to be designed for her course. She saw a lot of work before her and not a lot of time to do it. I told her about various levels of course design, referring to Boettcher & Conrad's continuum (2004), i.e. *Web-supported courses* (i.e. low-level design), *Web-centered courses* (i.e. medium-level design) and *Web courses* (i.e. high-level design). I explained to her that most of the professors I worked with had neither the time nor enough didactic resources to create complete Web courses. Consequently, their courses were more often than not simply Web-supported courses in the sense that they used the Web to post a variety of documents intended for student access. She explained to me that, while some of the readings she intended to use were already available on the Web, others would require taking into account copyright restrictions before posting. Moreover, she informed me that she had personal notes, guidelines, exercises, case studies, etc. which she wanted to post on her site. After this discussion, we did an inventory of her existing didactic resources, identifying what was missing and we set a calendar for producing the latter resources.

Following this discussion, we moved on to the readings she intended to post for her students and the usefulness of adding reading assignments for them. She said that she wanted her students to be able to draft their own reading reports without her having to supply an assignment, yet she knew that, by not providing one, they would likely spend precious time trying to figure out what to write and how to write it, time she felt could be better spent in their reading and "digesting" the course contents. To resolve the dilemma, we returned to the course objectives. Indeed, the objectives we had set aimed at their assimilating and applying the concepts presented rather than their simply analyzing the contents of the readings. The professor wanted students to be able to develop their own intervention strategy based on the principles discussed in the readings. The result was the realization that we should, if time allowed, provide students with some type of reading assignment to focus their attention on specific aspects of the content.

I believe that the design process has finally been proven successful because the professor seems to recognize the importance of developing course contents and learning activities based on set objectives. However, the objectives we set were far from being as developed as the three-component, performance-based objectives as prescribed by Mager (1997).[2] It appears unlikely that any professor would agree to take the time required to provide that level of detail. The most that I have managed to do is have them draft their general intentions and then provide a few details on specific objectives. Indeed, there is always resistance on their part to identifying objectives, even once they have identified their contents or subjects. However, a basic principle of instructional design requires the identification of objectives before any discussion of content (i.e. the means required to meet the objectives). Sometimes, I'm under the impression that ISD is almost an article of faith.

The subject of using videoconferencing to teach resurfaced because she found the idea particularly irritating. She told me she was in the habit of interacting frequently with her students, of "reading" their faces, and she feared that videoconferencing might interfere with her pedagogy. She expressed her uncertainties as well as her anger at a situation over which she had little control. (The university had negotiated an agreement to offer her course at a distance because before she had been hired.) I tried to encourage her by saying that, although V/C may indeed impose some limits on her pedagogical relationship with her students, there were certain advantages in using it, such as the possibility of reaching students located all over the province who would otherwise not be able to take her course. Moreover, given the fact that distance delivery would allow practicing professionals to attend her course, the depth of understanding which they would bring to debates and exchanges would most likely raise the level of dialogue in the classroom. These arguments seemed to carry the day.

The next subject to require our attention was how work was to be assigned to her students. She asked me what other faculty members were doing in their classes. I told her about different strategies implemented in higher education. In my view, there were four main strategies (see Figure 1). I used a schematic drawing to explain that some professors start their classes by requiring a considerable effort on the part of their students and then reduce the workload as the term unfolds (model A).

Other professors begin slowly, reach the maximum level of their course requirements by mid-term, then the workload tapers off (model B). Still others promote a more gradual approach, reserving the greatest workload for the latter part of the course (model C). Finally, some require about the same amount of work from students throughout the term (model D).

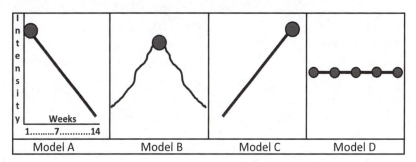

Figure 1: Diverse strategies for designing student workload

She considered that her expectations best fit model C, because she required her students to take a major test at the end of the course. We returned to her syllabus to ensure that this choice was reflected in her course activities and requirements between weeks 5 to 10. Having made these changes, we continued identifying objectives for these same weeks.

Session 5: Because the professor still felt ill at ease with the idea of videoconferencing, we began by continuing our conversation on what the medium would allow her to do and what it wouldn't. She was still not sure of how much time the Continuing Education department (CED), in charge of logistics, would give her and she was afraid of having to shorten class time because of the cost of using the V/C system. We decided that we needed more information from the CED to be sure that she could have as much videoconferencing time as she had when the course was offered on campus.

Now we broached the topic of "contact time" between professors and students (as one wag called it, "bums in seats") in a distance education context. We discussed instructional strategies vis-à-vis student needs in terms of real-time support, as in the model I presented to her during our first session.

Of course, as we all know, the "teaching" component of a lot of courses is often one-way oral transmission on the part of faculty, i.e. lecturing. However, in a distance education setting, a variety of documents, didactic resources and/or audio, video recordings provided to the students usually replace lectures. However, as we have seen, the problem faculty face in dual-mode universities is that there is rarely sufficient time or resources to develop quality mediatised resources. As a result, there is no clear distinction between teaching resources and learner support activities as there is in distance education courses developed by single-mode universities (such as TELUQ or Open). Hence, dual-mode university faculty tend to try to teach and provide learner support simultaneously (very much as they would on campus), using whatever two-way technology their institution has adopted that is available to them.

In this faculty member's case in particular, considering that her course was to start almost immediately and that there wasn't enough time to fully mediatise her course (as recommended by the design model I was using), we had to adopt a "design-light" approach, that is, something more like a traditional, on-campus course than a DE/Web course. Afterwards, once the course started, it might be possible to gradually mediatise it and to provide an increasing number of teaching resources online (such as recordings of her lecturing) while preserving real-time contact. In any case, this time, she would have to teach her course while providing learner support as she was used to doing in class. Doing so was possible with videoconferencing, but it was a departure from the classical DE model, a model which seemed increasingly inapplicable in the dual-mode university setting.

Since beginning work with this professor, I've not been able to establish a logical and orderly course design process and I haven't managed to apply the prescribed design model. Consequently, we seem to have entered an iterative cycle where nothing seems to get resolved and where the same elements, only partially treated, keep reappearing. I realize that it's because we have so little time to work together. It's like some odd "touch'n go" cycle. We start one thing and then, before we know it, we're off doing something else, only to have to go back to where we were. Panic seems to be gripping our small design team of two because time grows short and the course design requirements loom hugely unmet. The resulting pressure compels us to take shortcuts which eventually become a long and winding road, seemingly leading nowhere.

We then arrived at the topic of plenary sessions and how to organize them. The professor firmly intended to make certain her students did the required readings before coming to class. To make sure they did so, she planned to moderate weekly discussions during which she would ask students questions at random, in the hope of pressuring them to prepare themselves before coming to class. Afterwards, she would move on to the weekly case study which, in actual fact, was the same ongoing case study but simply another episode in the life of a fictitious professional experiencing a variety of problem-laden circumstances. I moved the conversation toward the degree of congruency which should exist between the way these sessions would be conducted and the overall course objectives. However, since we had not fully identified the specific objectives for the course, we had to return to the syllabus and together started drafting these for the plenary sessions. I emphasized that during these sessions she should aim at enabling her students to meet the highest-level objectives (i.e. the most difficult to attain in Bloom's taxonomy) whereas during the individual activities and the team activities, lower levels of cognition would likely be achieved. To make these sessions operational, we reorganized her syllabus by adding separate compartments for every objective. In this way, we could see exactly which objective would be met and when (i.e. during which activity).

The results of this session seems critical to the development of the model. Thus far, we have been unable to see the link between learning objectives and learning activities. Now, we are able to anticipate the required linkage and thereby develop the necessary resources. The syllabus grid is evolving into a planning tool, a natural outcome of the design model process. In fact, I see that a progression of sorts is occurring: where the model of course planning most widespread on campus is clearly faculty-centered, the model I have been promoting can best be described as design-centred. Now, as we move closer to student needs, a student-centred design model is emerging because it identifies the objectives to be reached, the activities necessary for their accomplishment as well as the resources that are made available to students. I think we are on more solid footing.

Session 6: We had now arrived at the point where continued identifying the objectives for the remaining weeks of the course. This was done with relative ease, considering the amount of work which had already been carried out. We were both keenly aware that these objectives would still have to be improved, i.e. to better represent the professor's real expectations with regard to her students, but we were satisfied with what we had accomplished.

With regard to the required linkage between current learning objectives and prior learning requirements, I explained the prerequisites testing (PT) concept to her, i.e. how the use of such a tool would allow her to determine out how well prepared her students were to take her course, before even starting it.

> *This is a design practice well anchored in corporate training, where every hour spent in training translates into bottom-line lost earnings, but there is rarely any implementation of such in higher education, simply because of the time and effort that would be required. Moreover, in higher education, students enrolled in programs of study may not need this since they always have to be eligible to enter a program and often have to take preparatory courses, two elements which diminish the need for front-end testing.*

She assured me that she always asked students questions at the beginning of her course to get to know them better and to get a feeling for their previous acquisitions. However, this was never done systematically. I explained to her how useful such tests are for students because PT identifies gaps in their instruction, thereby allowing professors to introduce them to palliative resources. We also discussed the Pre-test concept, the results of which indicate where students are situated on a continuum with regard to mastery of the objectives of the upcoming course. For instance, if some of her students have already mastered some of her course objectives, they could be given credit for such or be asked to contribute their time in helping their peers with those topics.

Now, we got to the subject that inevitably appeared once we had set up the basic structure of a course: the most difficult parts, the grey zones, or even the black holes (as I liked to call them). These were the parts of her course that gave a lot of students difficulty and produced the lowest test scores. We identified concepts arising from the most complicated theories seen in class that inevitably wreaked havoc among her students. We discussed various teaching strategies which might improve student understanding, such as using a visualization technique to simplify these abstract concepts.

> *Visualization is a highly specialized sub-domain of design which has numerous applications in fields as varied as physics, administration and physical education. However, extreme care must be taken when using visual representations of complex phenomena since there is, on the one hand, a danger of over-simplification. On the other hand, there is an advantage to be had through the judicious use of metaphor or analogy to help students grasp and retain various levels of complexity.*
>
> *I'm starting to see I need to develop a tutorial on using analogies and metaphors for educational purposes. I'll have to look at various educational software (such as Inspiration) to see what I can put together. I notice that, in a lot of courses, professors tend to rely overly on text to insure student learning. Some faculty naturally draw diagrams on the board in class but these drawings, quite useful in promoting student understanding, disappear with one wipe of the brush. According to Hodkins (2000); Mayer & Massa (2003); Prensky (2004); Reiber (1994) and www.visual-learners. com, visual learners, who are the natural products of a video game era, are increasingly populating our classes. To respond to them adequately, we need to supply the visual cues they need to process concepts. Such visual cues are as necessary to them as auditory cues were to an earlier generation.*

We started work on a very complex and abstract concept which was recurrent in her course and, as she explained it to me, I started doodling. Together, we fielded a variety of metaphors and analogies to try to find the one which best represented the professor's mental model. We both agreed that there were obvious limits to using a diagram and that it would be, at best, simply one expression among many which might be used to determine some of the parameters of any given concept. That said, it still represented, to a degree, the main aspects of the professor's current mental model. We then agreed that this graphically-represented concept (or graphic representation, or GR) we had developed should be presented with caution to students by first identifying its limits and by then emphasizing that it was but one representation of the concept in question. Nevertheless, the professor seemed to have gotten a lot out of this exercise and she said she was interested in developing others. We decided to put this GR into the hands of the technical support team so that they could professionally mediatise it, either in 2D or in 3D, animated or not.

As a person with a keen visual sense, I feel perfectly capable of developing such GRs and quite comfortable in doing so. This exercise seems to be crucial to the design of her course. I make a mental note to try to insert GR development as a permanent activity in the design process because it seems to allow professors to release themselves from their prejudices, to handle concepts freely and even to question them. I vaguely recall a saying of Plato to the effect that, to develop a concept, you must first start with a mental picture of that concept. However, it should be recognized that this can often be a destabilizing exercise for professors. But, after all is said and done, it is usually quite well received, a difficult but satisfying exercise. According to anecdotal student reactions to GRs, they seem to think it is one of the best didactic tools to have in a course.

While still working on the most difficult parts of her course, we discussed her ongoing case study, appearing in weekly episodes throughout the course. In her mind, it was geared to developing specific skills. So I asked her about the situations in each episode to ascertain to what extent each was based on real life.

I'm asking her this because I have doubts about how useful her ongoing case study will be in developing the skills she feels her students must develop. I feel I have to make sure that the professor, when drafting her scenarios, has not fallen into the domain of pure fiction.

I'm skating on thin ice and I know it. For an ID, this kind of manoeuvre is always delicate. As soon as the designer ventures into the domain (or should I say the den) of the professor, the barricades go up, dialogue becomes difficult and frustration is evident (on the part of the professor). This seems to be due to an impression, in the mind of the professor, that the ID has doubts about his/her competency as a subject matter expert. As an ID, I'm not aiming to do that but I feel that I have the duty to make sure that what is being presented to students is actually based on knowledge and not impressions. Consequently, by testing the quality of the information, the ID runs a risk of being accused of trying to wrest control of the design process from the professor, rather than doing what he or she has been paid to do: counsel the professor and design whatever the professor decides he/she wants designed. This, of course, reminds me of how rare the professor-ID tandem is in traditional universities where there are so few IDs compared to the number of professors. As a result, most professors have difficulty understanding the role and responsibilities of the ID, whose discipline is virtually unknown.

This session ended with a bit of stand-off. We both stuck to our guns and decided it was time to break for the day.

I'm thinking: "I must be nuts!" risking seeing the professor drop everything there and then after what may only amount, at best, to a Pyrrhic victory on my part. But this episode leaves me deeply troubled about the extent to which an ID must assume responsibility for his/her work. At what point does the professor's work become the ID's work? Is there a solid membrane separating the two… it doesn't feel that thick…

Session 7: At the request of the professor, we started discussing oral exams that her students have to take towards the end of the course. It became clear that, given the large number of students and the lack of time in class, she was going to have students team up for these presentations. Yet she maintained that every presentation would be individually marked, even though students would jointly present a single subject. They would have to divide it in two parts and each would take an equal part. A question loomed: how were we going to get students to divide up their presentations? She explained that she expected each team would present one theory from a list of theories that were all connected to her domain. I proposed she adopt a classic approach whereby one student would present the theoretical aspect and, the other student, the application of the theory with examples. She immediately opted for this approach and we started to establish a presentation calendar according to the amount of time available in class. The length of time assigned to each student was necessarily going to vary according to the number of students enrolled in the course. Using figures from earlier class enrolments (averages), we quickly put together a provisional schedule.

The professor then asked me to look at the objectives she had drafted between sessions to make sure that they expressed her true expectations. I noticed that she had several difficulties.

1. She used verbs such as "discuss, get acquainted, familiarize yourself with," when she should have chosen verbs indicating observable, measurable behaviours, as prescribed by Mager (1997).
2. She tended to describe what she does and drafted her objectives from her own point of view rather than identifying what she wanted her students to achieve and writing course objectives from their point of view.
3. She didn't distinguish between general objectives and specific objectives.
4. She had difficulty distinguishing between specific objectives and exam items.

As time was shorter than ever (her course was starting next week), we decided to return to the subject of student presentations. During the last working session, she had told me that she intended, during the first weeks of the course, to present the main theories of her domain. Then, she intended to ask her students to choose a theory from those that remained and present it. She justified doing this by saying that she wanted to be absolutely sure that they understood the fundamental theories in her field. As for the secondary theories, she said "they are less important."

Since Dewey, we know that when students are active participants in their own learning they have a better rate of acquisition (or of accommodation and assimilation according to Piaget, 1951, 1972) and that they demonstrate a higher level of competency (Gagné, 1985). I'm wondering why she thinks they will understand the theories she presents in lectures better than the theories they present after research and planning their own presentations...

In this regard, I asked if she thought her students would be more likely to master the main theories she would be presenting or the secondary theories they themselves would be presenting. We discussed the instructional consequences of this choice while examining other possible strategies. She agreed with me on two points:

a) The main theories were of the greatest importance in her course.
b) The students would likely have to master the theories they had been assigned in order to be present them adequately.

Beyond that, our ways parted when she insisted that, because she was responsible for the course, she must ensure that her students understood the fundamental theories. Consequently, she believed that it would be unprofessional to delegate this duty to her students. She said: "I am the most competent person to present these theories to them." This turned out to be a learning moment for me.

> The slightest insecurity on the professors' part can quickly degenerate into frustration and into a decline in enthusiasm for the design work which must be done. Most of the professors with whom I am working have never worked with an ID. Moreover, they rarely discuss pedagogy with their colleagues. As a result, when they begin the design process for the first time, some of them feel judged, reprimanded, depreciated (likely given the fact that they have no formal training in education, let alone design) and even threatened because of the instructional choices they espouse. The ID has to traverse these moments as a land mine removal expert would move about a minefield.

We returned to the question of presentations and I suggested a slightly less professor-led and more student participatory approach. She said she was perfectly all right with that. So we got to work on developing a scenario for one of the theories she would be presenting. We put some slides together with GRs illustrating various aspects of a given theory, adding questions here and there and inserting at times on-the-spot exercises for individuals or teams. The result was a presentation model which activated learning among students, required continuous class participation and highlighted concrete examples solicited from the participants. The situation had been defused. We even started having fun!

The very last subject we tackled was attitudes acquisition. She explained how her course aimed at helping students develop more than just theoretical knowledge, that is, it also had to help them develop a professional attitude. I relayed Gagné's (1985) position that attitudes are much harder to develop and take much more time to acquire than verbal information and intellectual skills.

> *Although her course is based on different theories which are supposed to have a direct application in her field, I wonder about how appropriate and to what extent they can be applied by her students. According to Gagné (1985), the acquisition of an attitude is only visible when one examines choices made by a person. I wonder how she will be able to examine choices made by her students since they will occur long after her course is over.*

According to the professor, no one theory was superior to any of the others. They all explained phenomena but from different points of view. As in any domain, certain theories applied in some circumstances better than they did in others. I asked her if she had ever wondered whether her students acquired said attitudes during her course or if they already had them before coming to class. We discussed this a bit and we arrived at the conclusion that it would probably be better if we drafted a series of objectives which dealt specifically with such things as scientific neutrality and unbiased application criteria.

This was the end of what had been, at times, a harrowing experience. There had been strife, tension and misunderstanding but we had achieved something: this course was a go.

Ex Post Facto Interview

On writing objectives: "How to write objectives, that was important learning. Everything got so much clearer; I've always written objectives but it's never been so clear!"

On developing team activities: "I have my students work in teams of two to better understand the material; work by twos allows students to confront and criticize one another's work...something that doesn't happen in class."

On developing an instructional strategy: "I see it happening in three stages; prior readings (chapter X), sharing (I ask them questions) and then students present chapter X et cetera. I supply them a[weekly] quiz to facilitate their understanding of the material."

On experiential learning and applying the weekly assignments concept: "Originally, we were going to develop weekly assignments based on various aspects of the schools of thought presented in class), on their analysis of and reflection on such. The readings provide the theory, the explanations I provide anchor the theory in real life and the weekly assignments foster student application of theory in their own lives. But it ends up being too much work to correct... then they are boring to correct!"

On the purpose of my instructional strategy: "I wanted to maximize the impact of the reading material by using weekly assignments linked to my course objectives to help them better integrate the course contents"... "I need a template or a model for my assignments, like a kind of universal reading-based assignment model which could be adapted to any kind of reading analysis."

On course delivery: "This course has never been taught at a distance but it's almost ready. But I don't see myself doing that. I don't like videoconferencing. If there was strong demand for the program, that would motivate me to deliver it at a distance. That would force me to further develop my assignments and my exercises. I think that a distance course makes you become more meticulous. If I did [if I offered my class at a distance, I would [likely] be satisfied with the results, with well-developed exercises but that would put me under a lot of stress." (Although this professor had been mandated by her department to deliver her course at a distance, she was obviously not at all sold on the idea. At the time of this interview, she was hoping to get a sessional to give her course.)

On plenary sessions and technology: "When you are with people, you start a conversation… a conversation can start with a question from a student"… "the non-verbal [the non spoken] is important."

On the importance of eye-to-eye contact: "We have to be able to hear each other; we don't have to see each other. A written exchange just doesn't cut it, it has no strength… the human voice is important to convey emotion, sarcasm, even irony."

On course delivery: "It's the technology that is a major obstacle, from what I've seen. Technical glitches… it looks like videoconferencing has a lot, it cuts out, it stops, it's just not reliable."

On control: "I have control over my presence in class but I have no control over the technology. Unless I'm sick, I am in class."

On teaching via distance education: "I believe in duty. If I was told that I had to do it, I would do it."

On whether she is motivated or not to teach via distance education: "No, I'm not. But, if it means teaching students in the developing world, yes. For us (in our province), I can adjust my schedule, even travel rather than use videoconferencing. (…). So long as I have audio, I'm OK. If it is reliable, OK I'll do it. I am so afraid that it won't work, that I waste my time and that lowers my motivation."

On design of her course: "It required a lot of my time, short-term, but [what we've produced] remains. I give three courses regularly and three others from time to time. (The regular ones) I work on them every year. I'm satisfied with this one [the one we worked on] but I want to do more. But I don't want to have to write up an assignment for each reading; I'll try to find another strategy."

On the future of her program with regard to distance education: "The future of the program delivered via distance education depends on the reliability of the technology…I can invest in teaching at a distance, I can allow myself to take risks…it's as though I was walking on a tightrope without a net below or, if there is one, it can be removed at any time. [Of course] I risk breaking my neck just as much in class...I have to be fully prepared but if there is a breakdown in technology, that just breaks my legs...it's kind of like when my classroom is locked, that gets me down. Technology is my safety net of sorts; it looks like it is getting better but, right now, it is not reliable."

Notes

1. See G. Kearsley's site on J. Bruner: http://tip.psychology.org/bruner.html and Jonassen's site: http://tiger.coe.missouri.edu/~jonassen/

2. Objectives development was in conformity with guidelines from the UNESCO site: http://www.unesco.org/webworld/ramp/html/r8810e/r8810e00.htm#Contents

CASE STUDY 4
GETTING OFF TO A GOOD START

Case Characteristics

While this case had some characteristics in common with the previous three, it also had some significant differences. These characteristics are summarized in the table below.

Table 9: Characteristics of the subject matter expert

Gender	Rank	Reason	Time	Availability	No. of sessions	K/ Design	K/ DE	GO/ SO
F	ASC	0	1	1	5	3	2	2

Gender: female

Rank: ASC = associate

Reason: O = organisational

Time-to-delivery: 1 = course already begun or is about to begin

Availability: 1 = minimally available (1-15 hrs)

Number of sessions = 5

Knowledge of Design 3 = advanced level

Knowledge of DE: 2 = tought three or more DE courses

General Obj. /Specific Obj.: 2 = GOs only

In terms of similarities to the three previous cases, this one also involved a female professor who was participating in the design process for organizational reasons. She faced the same time constraints as the others: her course was about to begin (1), she had little availability (1) and only five working sessions took place (5). In contrast to the previous three cases, this professor was at the mid-point in her career (ASC) and she had deep knowledge of instructional design (3) and of distance learning (2). Also significant was the fact that, like her colleagues, her reason for participating in the design process was organizational (O). This led her to view the design process as an additional obstacle in her already very busy schedule. She told me she wanted to "get it over with as quickly as possible." (I got an inkling of what it must feel like to be a dentist...). This statement set the tone for our work and constituted a significant constraining factor in the design of her course.

I had had the opportunity to work with this professor on other projects so at least that was running in our favour. She was in no way new to instructional design principles, having once used an earlier version of my model to construct a previous course. As for the case under study here, she already had a course syllabus because she had already taught this course on campus. However, by the time we met for the first time, the course was about to begin. Consequently, we had to start our design work by addressing the most problematic aspects of her course. As a result of her limited availability, we did not anticipate being able to meet more than four or five times.

Before our first meeting, I asked the professor, as usual, to send me a copy of her most recent course syllabus. I also picked up the other syllabi in her program and sent her a copy of the latest version of the working grid I had developed for Case 3.

Session 1: Our first meeting took place under stressful conditions. The professor was obliged to start teaching her course at a distance without the support she felt she required or the time to properly put it all together. This situation had resulted from the same type of university agreement discussed earlier, which the administration had been passed down to faculty a *fait accompli*. In addition, according to the professor in this case, the university had promised to provide pedagogical and technical support well in advance but had not done so. (According to another source, the professor had not asked to use the resources available.) Consequently, the course was about to begin without the professor being ready to deliver it at a distance, which had obviously engendered feelings of frustration on her part. As a result, she was quite on edge, which did not bode well for our upcoming work.

We began our session by reviewing her current course syllabus together. It was built according to the typical vertical pattern, containing a list of themes, bunched general objectives and compulsory readings. Having already studied it ahead of time, I pointed out that there were no specific objectives. The professor explained that she had not had time to write any but that she would like to do so. We therefore reorganized the general objectives, distributing them throughout her course and linking them to specific themes. Afterwards, we returned to the list of themes and identified, according to the proposed readings, sub-themes which would be studied in the course. This brought us closer to identifying the specific objectives.

Having identified the sub-themes for each week (of course, still in a provisional state), we returned to the series of readings proposed for each week. I noticed that there were too many readings for some weeks and an insufficient number for others. Seeing as she had brought all the readings along with her (copies of all her texts and articles), I proposed we go through them and reassess her weekly redistribution, perhaps reordering them from most to least important. I then asked her to tell me about the contribution of each text to her students' learning and their meeting her course objectives. As she explained the relevance and importance of each, I was able to jot down a list of potential specific objectives, which we then analyzed and modified accordingly. Where there were too many texts for a given week, I asked her which texts were essential and which ones, although interesting, were not absolutely necessary. I wanted to find out which ones linked up with the objectives and which ones did not. We got through her readings and established a quantitative limit of 50 to 75 pages of readings per week for the easier texts and a 25- to 35-page limit for the more difficult ones. This task was difficult and tedious for the professor but she was aware that it was important because she knew that she had not distributed the readings to suit her student's cognitive processing capacity. Our session ended with my explaining a method for identifying specific objectives (see below).

In cases where professors have difficulty writing out their specific objectives (SO) but where they already have student performance assessment instruments (i.e. tests, exams) developed, I recommend, as mentioned, "reverse engineering" (see Figure 2), that is, writing SOs which are derived from exam items.

In cases where a course has already been taught, professors have exams, exercises, assignments or projects with specific guidelines. These assessment instruments are the end-product of the instructional process and, consequently, representative of a professor's true intents and thus indicative of his or her specific learning objectives. Using performance criteria as it appears in the exam items, one can then establish, by induction, a course's specific objectives. Reading through the exams, it becomes a matter of identifying the specific objective targeted by a given question. As specific objectives are more general than objective exam items (Morissette, 1984), some of these exam items usually have to be grouped together to be able to identify a given specific objective. However, when it comes to items which are more subjective, each item may target either a general objective (GO) or several SOs. (The more objective items are usually simple test items such as multiple-choice questions while the more subjective are "complex production" questions (Scallon, 1988) or essay questions.)

As can be seen in Figure 2, closed-end exam items depend on specific objectives; that is, they are always written on the basis of a given SO. For open-ended exam items, such a claim cannot be made because the item can, in the case of an essay question, often equate to a general objective.

The guidelines for individual or team assignments are often another source for specific objectives. Of course, as with exam items, these guidelines are usually too precise to be turned into an objective per se; however, some extrapolation is usually possible.

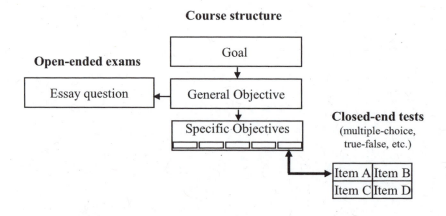

Figure 2: Writing specific objectives using reverse engineering

Session 2: At the professor's request, this session began with a discussion of the way in which she intended to evaluate her students' performance. She had already identified, in a general manner, the assignments on which students were to be evaluated.

Assessment instruments / Marking Scheme

Assignment 1: Critical summary of a text	20 %
Assignment 2: Team project on (...)	20 %
Assignment 3: Creativity project on (...)	15 %
Individual Assignments	30 %
Team Assignments	15%

Continuing on from the previous session, it was now time for her to clarify a certain number of elements in her course, including the nature of the activities and assignments she had planned as well as their integration into the course schedule. After some discussion, we thus decided that assignments 1, 2 and 3 would be due in Weeks 5, 10 and 14. As for the individual reading reports, I suggested writing out a mix of open-ended and closed-ended questions to guide students through the ideas presented in the weekly readings. As for the team assignments, I proposed writing a series of open-ended questions of several types, including factual, inference and application questions. These types of questions target discussion and negotiation of meaning in a constructivist sense (Jonassen et al., 1999) and encourage hierarchical knowledge assimilation (according to Gagne, Briggs & Wagner, 1986). Each individual assignment would be worth 3 points and each team report would be worth 1.5. Students would send their completed assignments to the professor each week by email and she would mark and return them by email. She later decided that, to decrease the amount of email she would have to handle, students would simply deposit them in the Assignments box on the course website.

Dividing up points in this way is a double-edged sword: it may encourage diligence on the part of the student and result in more structured learning but it also requires meticulous follow-up by the professor. The issue of finding the right balance comes up frequently in instructional design. On the one hand, most professors want to offer a quality, structured course to students as well as provide them with a high level of learner support in the form of written and verbal feedback. On the other hand, they are usually overwhelmed with research- or service-related tasks and responsibilities. Providing higher levels of structure in their courses as well as offering quality learner support while meeting research-related commitments is illustrative, for many faculty members, of King Solomon's dilemma.

We then discussed how teams would be formed in her course. We decided that students should chose their own teams of between two to five members (depending on course enrolments) and that they should meet at least once a week to exchange information on the individual & team assignments. A spokesperson would be appointed for each week of class who would then be called upon to summarize their findings in class. A general discussion led by the professor would follow.

We then decided to look at her assignments and the questions therein based on her required readings to see how much "retrofitting" would be required. To simplify matters somewhat (considering that her course was about to begin and she felt that writing out questions would be time-consuming), I told her that her questions could take the form of a weekly quiz, using the quiz tool in the LMS. I reminded her that, while closed-end questions took longer to develop than open ones, they could be correctly automatically, which would save time during course delivery. As went through her readings, we thought of questions, knowing we could refine them later. After one hour, using some of her original questions, we had written the alternatives (the distracters plus the right answers) for her first quiz. She felt confident she would be able to develop further quizzes, even if it meant doing so while her course was in progress, by keeping a week ahead of the students. She said she would write the questions up and ask the Instructional Development Coordinator (IDC)to post them on her website, at least until she learned how to do so herself.

This reminds me of rapid prototyping *(Tripp & Bichelmeyer, 1990) and just-in-time instruction (Schank, Berman & Macpherson, 1999), two concepts prevalent in design literature. The possibility of developing a quiz on-the-fly for immediate posting on the Web via an LMS has opened up new possibilities for professors who, because of their numerous professional responsibilities, often do not have enough time to do as much planning (front-end design) as they would like. The advantage of using an LMS is that they can develop and modify assessment instruments at the last minute; the disadvantage is, because they can do it at the last minute, they often do and the result is, at times, less-than-adequate instruments for evaluating student performance.*

Towards the end of this working session, we began developing a series of open-ended questions for the team assignment based on the same reading, which took us about half an hour. It was not very difficult given the fact that the professor was very familiar with her readings and knew which questions she wanted to ask, having asked them orally in previous courses. She now had models to follow to develop other individual- and team-oriented assignments.

Session 3: I returned to her course syllabus and asked how far she had gotten in writing her objectives. She told me that she didn't intend to write them because she felt that the questions in the reading assignments were sufficiently detailed and that the students would easily understand what they were expected to do each week. She also told me that she was completely overwhelmed with other work and that writing objectives was not a priority for her.

> *This unwillingness to write objectives is not new: I found it in the previous three cases. I believe that this type of reaction is, considering a professor's workload, perfectly normal and understandable. I am starting to wonder to what extent Dick & Carey's theoretical model (1990–2007) takes into account how course design is done in the "real world" of higher education. The approach proposed by D&C is quite prescriptive, stringent and precise. Either you adhere to it or you don't. As mentioned, Tessmer & Wedman (1990) speak of "layers of necessity" in design, that instructional systems are to be developed according to what is required of them; that is, one can, as painters do, put on an additional "layer" (i.e. coat of paint) or not! As an instructional designer, I constantly find myself in situations where I am forced to make compromises, maybe even betray basic design principles to some degree, just so that I can move forward with the process. Why? Because we live in a world where not everything goes according to plan, and sometimes things happen for no apparent reason, quite simply because we have neither the time nor the means to make sense of it all, to make it conform to the standards of our profession. It seems an ID's work and degree of influence have always been and will always be reliant on his or her working environment. As I've mentioned, IDs are still a novelty in dual-mode universities and no one really seems to know who they are, what they do or how they fit in with everyone else involved. In their quest to improve the quality of the instructional process, they must "brave the high seas" of higher education, all the while being careful not to make too many waves in the process. Quite the challenge indeed. Consequently, I have come to envisage design as an iterative process, which can be incrementally*

improved, but which is always ipso facto *incomplete, imperfect and fragmentary.*

At the professor's request, we moved on to discussing the creativity assignment that she wanted her students to do. She intended to give them complete freedom. (As an ID, I had concerns about the "complete" part.) We discussed various project guidelines which would give them this freedom but also provide basic guidelines (which would make her marking easier). I suggested several assessment instruments such as log books, scrapbooks (a photo album or texts, artefacts, etc.) or portfolios, ideally virtual, which would allow students to reflect on the knowledge they had acquired, while drawing upon the texts they read and weekly discussions with their peers. They would be able to piece together associated elements which came to mind or which were illustrative of a key concept or of a practical application of a given theory, as seen in class. Since her students were, for the most part, working professionals in her field, she felt that this type of activity would be highly beneficial to them.

In my experience, this type of exercise is indeed valuable because it encourages students to draw upon their own personal experience to complete a task, which in turn requires them to internalize their reflection. Afterwards, they discuss what they've done with the group and this prompts an even higher level of knowledge construction. This reflection came to me as a visual representation, that of a swimmer who dives deep to speed along, then comes to the surface for air. In the same way, the learner introspectively dives deep within, and then comes up to share what she or he has found with the group. Later, I drew a GR of this idea, reproduced below (Figure 3).

We then moved on to discuss team assignments, the advantages and disadvantages of having them, and the ideal way of developing them. Earlier, we thought that teams should be made up of 2 to 5 students depending on the numbers enrolled. Here again, we faced what was ideal versus what was feasible. According to the professor, teams of two worked the best, yet small teams meant more teams for her to manage and more marking, follow-up, and assignment structuring. I concurred; there was a trade-off to be made. In the end, we agreed on a maximum of 6 teams of 3 students (since this was a graduate course). If there were more than 18 enrolments, we would increase the number of students per team, as needed.

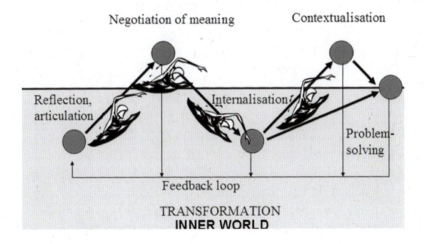

OUTER WORLD
COMMUNICATION

Figure 3: Moving between the inner world of transformation and the outer world of communication

Note to self: what is best for students is not necessarily what is best for faculty. This case shows the importance of balancing the needs of students with the limits of faculty (see Figure 4). Students hope for ideal learning conditions just as much as professors hope for ideal teaching conditions. The only solution is to find some middle ground which insures acceptable conditions for all. Indeed, finding this fair and equitable "middle ground" seems to me to me to be one of the biggest challenges in higher education.

The professor then asked me how to distribute the workload required of her students. I explained the four basic models I had observed faculty used (see Figure 1) and I recommended she consider either model B (assignments start out slowly, build to a summit towards the middle of the course, then gradually decrease the requirements) or Model D (a steady level of assignments required of students and a corresponding level of marking by faculty). To sum up, given her decision to have weekly assignments and to allocate points for them throughout the term, model B seemed to be the most advantageous to students and faculty.

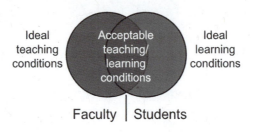

Figure 4: Ideal teaching vs. ideal learning conditions: The challenge of finding a middle ground

The professor then asked me how to distribute the workload required of her students. I explained the four basic models I had observed faculty used (see Figure 1) and I recommended she consider either model B (assignments start out slowly, build to a summit towards the middle of the course, then gradually decrease the requirements) or Model D (a steady level of assignments required of students and a corresponding level of marking by faculty). To sum up, given her decision to have weekly assignments and to allocate points for them throughout the term, model B seemed to be the most advantageous to students and faculty.

To promote student involvement in the course and in the hopes of sustaining enrolments (based on one of Moore & Kearlsey's (2004) numerous and useful recommendations), I suggested that she require that a weekly assignment be handed in during the initial weeks of the course and that she provide immediate feedback to students with regard to that assignment. An added advantage of this was that students would be free, towards the end of the course, to concentrate more time and effort on their artistic project.

At this point, the professor asked how she would conduct her plenary sessions and the linkage between individual and team activities. I explained that, according to the design model we were using, the plenary sessions were primarily aimed at learner support: a time for direct dialogue between professor and students, rather than a time for lecturing. The aim of the selected readings and the assignments they were to complete, either alone or in teams, before to coming to class were to prepare them for the plenary session. I also explained that if she had a PowerPoint presentation to which she would like to add a soundtrack, all she had to do was get the Instructional Development Coordinator to show her how to do it. She could even do this from her own work station. Afterward recording her sound track, she could send it to him and he would upload it to her website. In this way, she would be able to provide her students with a valuable teaching resource before to her plenary sessions. That would allow them to access her lecturing at a time of their choosing. By proceeding in this manner, more class time (via videoconferencing) could be spent discussing and deepening their knowledge of key concepts through questions and answers. I then showed her an example of a PowerPoint presentation with a soundtrack I had done myself.

> *I have already used* RealPresenter, Camtasia, *and then* Captivate *on numerous occasions, such as when preparing tutorials for faculty development. Having a collection of PPT slides ready, I sit down at my work station, put on my headset and record the soundtrack. If I'm not satisfied with my presentation, I can go back over any portion of it and edit it. After that, I save it in an accessible format (such as* QuickTime *or* Windows Media Player*) and add it to my website. There it would remain unless I needed to revise it, at which time I would open the original document, make my changes and then save and post the new version. Again, the main advantage I see here is a shift from reliance on purely synchronous mode (via videoconferencing) to the availability of both synchronous- and asynchronous-based resources. An activity which was previously only available to participants in a session was now accessible asynchronously to anyone to whom access was given. The addition of this kind of didactic resource meant that faculty could, in theory, now devote more time in synchronous mode with their students (during weekly videoconferencing-enabled sessions) to discussion and interaction rather than to lecturing. Of course, they still had to find time to do the recording but, once it was done, it was money in the bank. I could feel a sea change was in the making.*

The professor concurred that this arrangement allowed for a better distribution of activities and she eagerly looked forward to the possibility of having more time to devote to discussions with her students. As for her fear of not having the time to prepare her slide presentations and record soundtracks, I explained that all she had to do was simply take matters one week at a time. Every resource she developed was an investment in her course that could be used over and over, or edited as required. Moreover, the coordinator would be there to help her during her initial recordings. She already had several PowerPoint slides on the course's contents that she had made the previous year. The stress, like fog—the fog of design—was starting to lift.

Session 4: During this working session, the professor returned to the idea of developing PPT slides and recording soundtracks for her students to listen to before the plenary sessions. She stated that these PPT presentations would allow students to complete the individual and team activities more effectively. She expressed her growing interest in doing things this way and said she had a number of anecdotes she liked to share with students in class. Such anecdotes allowed students to get a better understanding of contextual factors involved in a given subject as well as benefit from the experience of others but these were often among the first things to be omitted when of class time was short. Since a significant portion of her teaching could now be done before she even saw the students in class each week, she now hoped to be able to reincorporate these undocumented anecdotes and real-life stories into her plenary session discussions.

The professor then wanted to discuss her weekly readings and the general manner in which her course contents were presented. She explained that as her course was based on certain basic, underlying concepts, she had anchored it in the idea of *organic emergence*. The whole course revolved around this notion, presented in the form of a tree diagram that illustrated the evolution, interaction, mixing and the relative position of these concepts with respect to others as well as the schools of thought from which they had sprung. Where did these concepts come from? What had been their influence on such and such a time and place? Where are we at now in terms of these concepts? What about these concepts in the United States and Europe? Because the course had a significant historical component, we began exploring different means of representing these concepts visually to facilitate their acquisition by her students. Some of the concepts, she felt, were difficult for students to grasp.

I proposed a diagram on the origin and progression of one of these key concepts, seeing it as a stream meandering through rough terrain, meeting with various obstacles and subsequently branching off at various places. We pictured it meeting up with other streams (or concepts) to form a river, at times forming a lake but eventually joining a bigger river which finally flowed into the ocean. This metaphor appeared to convey the evolution of the key concepts in question and the professor, having never seen anything like it before, was extremely happy with it. We pictured developing other analogy-inspired GRs such as the pyramid (to illustrate the effect of building from the ground up) and the iceberg (to show how, in one of her concepts, one part is visible to the user whereas a larger part is hidden). In doing so, we came to understand the degree to which higher-level objectives ("cognitive strategies" according to Gagne) could be promoted using GRs that would be discussed during plenary sessions. I explained to her the GR's pedagogical role as one type of *advance organizer* (Ausubel, 1963); i.e. how a diagram can serve as a mental model (Gentner, 1983) and open up a path, through visualization, to a higher level of understanding. This discussion led to another, i.e. the link, at least in my mind, between activity types (individual, team and plenary) and Bloom's (1984) taxonomy of learning behaviours (see the pyramid analogy-inspired Figure 5 below). At the end of this session, I explained to her that, by building a course syllabus in such a way that individual activities feed into team activities which then feed into plenary sessions, she would be constructing a hierarchy of learning activities & events that would likely improve knowledge construction "through layering" for her students.

> *"Layering" here is used in a Tessmer & Wedman (1990) sense (as in "layers of necessity"), meaning that students move from one layer of activities (developed according to their needs but also in taking into account available resources) to the next (i.e. from an individual activity to a team activity to a plenary session activity), the latter always being more complex in terms of interaction (Anderson, 2008) than the former.*

Another important skill that she wanted her students to acquire was related to ICT technical ability, to wit, mid-level mastery of PowerPoint. The burgeoning integration of ICT into the professional environments where her students were working or would be working was of such high importance that she decided to make it a general objective of her course. We discussed this objective's impact on team creation and team activities. She made a mental note to inform teams that they should include at least one student who had working knowledge of this software. For the more experienced students, a general objective related to helping train other students was added, specifically for them. She planned to offer a certain incentive to those students who accepted to do this, perhaps the omission of an assignment or some other element to be determined during the course.

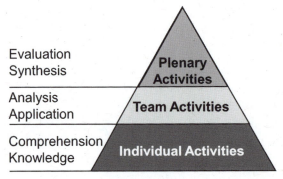

Figure 5: Bloom's cognitive domain taxonomy in relationship to course activities

Session 5: With her teaching strategies for the most part established and with a few initial assessment instruments identified, even partially developed, we began this session by talking about student support strategies and what means were available to her. Because the course was being offered at a distance, the professor was worried about her ability to support her students in the way she was used to doing. Aside from weekly videoconferencing and email, she had not thought of any other ways. At that point, I suggested she set up an online discussion forum in the LMS. A discussion forum would enable her to lead a discussion in asynchronous mode and allow her students to interact and support one other. She told me that forums were something she had heard about but had never used. In terms of added workload, she was not exactly sure what implementing one would entail. She also inquired about using the chat function. I explained the difference between using a forum and a chat and then took her to a site with discussion forum in which I was a participant. There I was able to show her how a forum actually worked and what it might involve in terms of commitment. We then toured a chat site, the workings of which I also explained. I also informed her that, pedagogically speaking, the forum was by far the more useful tool of the two because users could access it at a time convenient to them. Chatting, on the other hand, required a real-time presence by users, making it more difficult to arrange. Pedagogically speaking, chat sessions also had the potential to become quite chaotic when more than a handful of people participated.

We then returned to the forum in which I was a participant. It was a small forum of about 40 participants, mainly designers. I explained that some people posted messages more frequently than others. In addition, participation seemed to depend in large part on the subject being debated. I explained that it was a good way to get students to communicate among themselves, to encourage them to help each other out and, quite simply, to have them interact (Fahy, 2003). Moreover, she could use the site as a kind of bulletin board for her course. She was interested in the bulletin board idea but, as for the forum itself, she was afraid of simply not having enough time to participate in it regularly. Nonetheless, she did find the idea of a weekly debate so interesting that she decided to write out and post a series of questions on weekly course readings, to serve as potential topics for debate. Even though she would only look in on discussions as her schedule permitted, she felt that this would hopefully promote a heightened level of peer-to-peer interaction. She also saw that, for some teams, the forum could also be a way to carry out certain team assignments. Indeed, each team, in addition to having access to the general forum, also had the possibility of setting up a forum intended for its own members only.

The virtual discussion forum, despite the fact that it is rapidly becoming a well-established fixture in higher education and one of the Internet's true gems, is nevertheless, pedagogically speaking, a new medium for a lot of faculty members, especially for more senior professors. The forum fulfills a need which has long existed in distance learning: for students to establish a group identity and exchange freely with one another without space-time constraints. Of course, in order for it to work, the forum requires active participation, ideally, of all students as well as their ongoing involvement throughout the course. I have also found that, unless forums are organized according to set themes (threads), debates can become chaotic and unbeneficial to students. One final drawback to the forum is this: most of the professors with whom I have worked have never used a forum (even fewer have used a chat tool, not to mention a wiki or a blog). What's more, they have neither the interest nor the time (the lack of the former seems to be due to a lack of the latter) to learn how to use/manage a forum. This brings up the whole issue of faculty development in IT, their growing needs versus their severe time constraints and the conflicts involved therein.

A further note on the forum's synchronous mode counterpart—the chat—as I mentioned, I don't see any valuable pedagogical application for it, especially when large groups are involved. It does of course enable two or three individuals to interact quite effectively as a small team; however, in my experience, once the group reaches four or five, dialogue tends to become quite disorderly, confused and difficult to follow. For this reason, I do not encourage its use in officially-sanctioned activities. On the other hand, now that we have tools like MSN and Skype for multiple, online audio discussions, written chatting seems already to be a thing of the past, a short-lived technical innovation which has come and gone, almost overnight.

We continued on with a discussion on her using the synthesis grid for the presentation of her course, her course activities as well as her course schedule. As mentioned, her syllabus, at that point, was based on the vertical pattern, with no clear indication of what students were expected to do each week. After studying the grid, she agreed to use it. We then began transferring the components of her course directly into the grid. As we did this, it instantly became clear what activities would take place each week. At the same time, we were also able to identify empty spots where extra activities would have to be developed. After talking things over, I recommended putting her grid directly online, i.e. creating a Web site for her course on the institution's online platform so that it could be used as the home page for her course. We would then be able to set up direct hyperlinks between the grid and digital documents such as readings or student assignments. She told me that she would talk with some of her students to see what they thought about the idea and get back to me. I made a note to ask the Instructional Development Coordinator to post a grid on a test site and set up some hyperlinks to a few texts and documents so that she could try it out the next time we met.

As I mentioned, the synthesis grid is structured quite differently from traditional course syllabi, which are mainly vertical. The course is not divided into modules or units of unspecified duration but is strictly linked to the actual time available for each class period: one week. As with most courses, the one under development was a typical 3-credit course, giving it a maximum "seat time" of 45 hours, spread over 15 weeks. The grid was thus divided horizontally into columns identifying the various course components (objectives, content and activities: individual, team and plenary), displayed along the horizontal axis to create a continuous link between every component. Vertically, the grid was divided into temporal units corresponding to each weekly class. This continuous link along the horizontal axis is usually missing in the traditional course syllabus, or the vertical course syllabus, as I like to call it.

The connection between design theory and its implementation which resulted in my developing a working grid seems to me perfectly natural. I have already decided to abandon the original design model in favour of this grid, which seems to better assist professors in their thinking and course planning. Indeed, I'm noticing that course design activities have really started to take off. Another thing I've noticed is that I've stopped calling the grid a synthesis grid (rather awkward to begin with) preferring to label it a "horizontal course syllabus" (HCS).

In hindsight, I see that the precise distinction that I sought to make between so-called teaching, learning and assessment activities was mostly of theoretical interest rather than universal interest to faculty and seemed to even represent an obstacle in the design process. From now on, I intend to speak to professors about the horizontal course syllabus (see Figure 6), placing particular emphasis on the development of weekly activities and linking specific objectives, individually, and content to such. In doing so, we will be able to concentrate on developing activities one week at a time.

As I forge ahead through the process of migration from on-campus teaching activities towards course design, development and delivery at a distance, I am becoming aware of faculty's fundamental need to uphold the same academic standards and maintain the same flow of activities to which they are accustomed with a traditional on-campus course. For instance, a professor is typically willing to spend approximately three hours per week "delivering content" and he/she expects students to carry out about six hours of study outside of class, either individually or in teams or a combination of both. This adds up to a total of nine hours of activities per week for a regular 3-credit course. In light of this crucial factor: time, I am now starting to see the implications of such on a larger scale and to better envisage the activities involved:

- the in-class "teaching activities" from the professors' point of view: the three hours of weekly "seat-time" corresponds to the various activities estimated to take faculty and students approximately three hours to complete during a plenary session, such as faculty- or student-led discussions, debates, in-class assignments, etc.
- the before-class "learning activities" from the students' point of view: the estimated six hours of various activities that students are expected to complete and which could include: compulsory readings (books, articles or lecture notes) which the professor has provided to students, either as a hard copy or electronically; individual or team exercises to be completed based on course readings or on Web sites; online discussion forums, listserv-, email- or forum-based messages to be written and consulted; PowerPoint-based lectures, possibly with a soundtrack, and including other elements such as 2D or 3D animations; other audio (MP3s) or digital video Internet-based documents (YouTube), etc.

A few months have passed now since I asked the head IDC to look into finding publishers who already have ebook versions of their books (or parts of them). I also asked him to explore the possibility of reaching an agreement with other publishers who had none on digitalizing texts and posting them on the Web (in a secure mode, of course, protected on the asynchronous platform by password-controlled access). In that way, students would only have to pay for a subscription to a given book, or even a part of a book, rather than having to buy a paper copy. Moreover, this type of arrangement would be great for professors because they often wish to use only one chapter in a given book. They would be able to customize their course readings and have students pay for a subscription to that chapter. Initial findings by the

IDC has turned up a few publishing houses which appear to offer some of their books in a digital format and even allow faculty to extract chapters here and there and thereby compile their reading list. Others, however, appear to have never even heard of such a possibility (especially French-language publishing houses); still others have even expressed hostility (in some cases, scarcely-veiled threats) to the very idea. For books whose intellectual property rights have expired or those which are already in the public domain (i.e. government publications, etc.), it appears one is free to use them without having to worry about copyright issues.

The role of publishers, publications, and property rights seem seems poised for revision as knowledge becomes more globalized and increasing pressure is exerted by the public to have free access to it, especially to research findings published by academics that, directly or indirectly, are paid with tax dollars.

The Horizontal Course Syllabus Grid

Course title: _____	Faculty _____
Course number : _____	Department _____
Professor Contact Information	Program _____
Name: _____	Calendar: Start _____ End: _____
Phone number:_____ Fax: _____	Website: www.youruniversity.edu
Email: _____	Virtual Classroom site: www.yourvirtualu.edu
Office location: _____	Weekly classes on _____
Office hours:	From ____ to ____ .

Main objective(s)   Understand the terminology and concepts linked to ……

Specific Objectives	Content or Themes	Individual Activities	Team Activities	Plenary sessions
- Define...	- Definitions...	Read Taylor (2005) View Richey (2009)		
- Identify...	- Roles...	Complete Form 1A		
- Explain...	- Consequences		Contribute to the forum. Complete Exercise 1B	
- Summarise...	- Overview...			Present team findings.

Figure 6: The horizontal course syllabus grid

The prospect of providing readings to students directly from her own website seemed to delight the professor. I explained to her that this was still fairly virgin territory and that agreements had first to be put in place. Nonetheless, having digital versions of readings would allow her students to use a full arsenal of flexible word processing tools such as the search tool, also those for the visually-disabled (that can change font size or screen configuration). She agreed that this option was most promising. Due to time constraints, however, we both agreed that it would be something to be gradually integrated into her course, but she would use paper copies this time.

This subject led us into a discussion of copyright law, intellectual property and the readings she intended to use, some of which were written by authors she knew personally. I asked if she had ever contacted these authors (or other professor in her field) to find out what courses they taught, if they taught the same courses she did and whether they'd be interested in sharing materials. She told me that, aside from a few brief conversations on teaching at various conferences, she had never contacted her colleagues systematically about teaching resources. I mentioned how professors are increasingly creating focussed learning communities and blending their efforts to produce didactic material and learning objects which they can then share with one another (such as Merlot, www.merlot.org). I explained that such collaboration could greatly reduce overall preparation time for everyone involved and, through peer review, could also improve the quality of resources produced.

Indeed, an increasing number of collaborative activities are underway, such as open access publication of books and journals, and they are being carried out entirely online, thereby offering several significant advantages:

1. *It speeds up publication time;*
2. *It removes distribution problems (especially if it is published in Open Access mode (http://www.doaj.org/), such as with a Creative Commons license http://creativecommons.org/);*
3. *It makes document updating much easier. In fact, a book could be a permanent work-in-progress; that is, as it was being read and critiqued (as feedback was provided to authors), it could be constantly updated;*
4. *It would receive a far larger peer review than what is currently possible.*

The professor immediately saw the advantage of establishing contacts with her peers about online publishing and freely sharing resources and she said it was something she intended to do. I told her that she could even create a forum for professors who taught the same course across Canada, North America or anywhere in the world. This discussion invigorated us, elevated our vision and inspired us to move on and complete what was left in the design of her course.

She raised the issue of guest speakers that she would often invite to her course and problems that inevitably cropped up every year due to various turns of events, such as sickness, dangerous winter driving conditions, etc. If a guest were to not show up on the planned class date, she would have to completely change everything. She asked me how technology could help her. Since her course was, at least for the time being, being delivered via videoconferencing, I simply proposed the idea of, from now on, her having guest speakers come to the nearest videoconferencing location. The advantage of doing this was a) it would mean the guest wouldn't have to travel too far, and b) that the talk could be taped and archived for future use. However, this arrangement would most likely add an extra cost to the course, depending on the speaker's location.

I considered getting my university to subscribe to a synchronous, desktop teleconferencing platform which would allow speakers to participate in her class, regardless of where they were, without even having to leave their office or home. Furthermore, she would not have to restrict her choice of speakers based on travel costs. By having access to a Web-based, synchronous platform, she could invite people from anywhere in the world to speak to her class, show slides and field questions from students. If time zones were an issue, she could decide to interview the person using the synchronous platform, record it, and then either play it during a given plenary session or stream it from her web site where students could view it before the next plenary session. This would require further research and arm-twisting too because use of the V/C system was being subsidized and it had originally cost an arm and a leg. So it had to be used.

Another problem that the professor brought up was her students' lack of access to scientific journals. She was aware that, in her field of study, some journals were available online but that she had never had the time to look into the matter further. She was also leery of the quality of such journals. We immediately started an Internet search to find out how many peer-reviewed, virtual journals there were, especially those which were free. At the same time, I also asked the reference librarian to make up a list of journals in this professor's field of study to see to which ones were in our library. Together, we managed to identify three relevant (in which authors she recognized were published) scientific journals, including one recently-launched journal and another that required a password which could be obtained upon payment of a modest, annual membership fee. The professor told me that, with everything we had found, her students should be capable of carrying out some top-notch work. (Her interest and enthusiasm were starting to peak!)

Our working sessions ended with this one. Not everything was done and there were still quite a few loose ends to be tied up but I was confident that she would see things through. I just hoped that she would find time to finish off those parts of the work that we had not had time to complete.

Ex Post Facto Interview

On the design process and using the horizontal course syllabus (HCS): "It was the first time I had ever used this kind of syllabus model. Usually, I provide information about my course "vertically" as you say. I describe how the course is put together, assessment, etc. The first thing I did this time was tidy things up, particularly in the weekly readings. That allowed me to see what was not working...like weeks where there was too many or too few readings. That then helped me see the link between each of my objectives and each of my readings. As a result, I dropped some of the readings which were interesting but not really essential so that I could focus more on what was essential. It was important that I base things directly on the objectives for that week. So those readings I kept as well the most important activities, like the ones which helped students meet the weekly objectives. Overall, I'd say that I managed to remove about 25% of non-essential readings and activities."

On student participation: "The only way to make sure that students do the assigned reading is to give points. I don't know whether they actually did them before, but with the horizontal course syllabus, I decided to organise things differently and only keep the readings which were directly linked to my objectives, just to make sure that students would do the reading. I then used the idea of creating question-based assignments from your model so that they could get the most possible out of the readings. With the HCS, the readings I kept were all compulsory. As I said, I also added points for each assignment. Overall, this is what I did:

- tidied up the course readings and activities;
- added a reading assignment (like a grid) which helped students work with the readings more effectively;
- made all of the readings compulsory

The results of this started to show during in-class discussions and debates. The discussions were more enriching as we would relate ideas to the texts and go into them a lot deeper. Some students told me that other professors would ask them to do required readings but then they would never bring them up in class afterwards, at least not in any consistent manner. When using the HCS, congruency is a must. If a professor provides students with texts, if the texts are indeed important, then it is just as important to go through them and analyze them together. The HCS made it (my course) so much more systematic."

On the design process: "What impact has it had on my teaching? Well, for starters, I find the HCS useful, whether I teach at a distance or not. It works irrespective of how I teach. Some students recommended the HCS to my colleagues. It is so clear. That helps a lot. For instance, right now, I am giving a course at another university, team teaching with a colleague... but we didn't use the HCS to organize the course. I had been unable to participate in the development of the course syllabus and now I'm having a hard time figuring out the reasoning in how the course is put together. With the HCS, you can see how, from week to week, things are linked...you just fill in the blanks. With the other (course) plan, I have only a vague idea of what we are doing each week. It's hard to go back to the old way of doing things."

On individual or team activities: "That's how I learned to do things. Is it because I have been teaching for a long time that I know it is important? I do know that team activities enable learning. Even when I was doing my Master's and PhD, I had team projects to do. With my undergrad students, there are problems within teams with regard to sharing the work, but not with my Master's students. I tell them that, when they graduate, "you are going to work in teams so it is important to learn how to do so now." At the undergraduate level, students often see teamwork as something unnecessary and too time-consuming, especially because a lot of them already have jobs. They simply want to get their degree and get a full-time job. I have to remind them that team work is part of their learning."

On technology and faculty: "I really didn't have time to put my course online (in the LMS). You have to do it ahead of time. Besides, my students weren't ready to use it anyway. In the end, I dropped the idea and we simply posted everything on an ordinary web page with links to downloadable documents. The LMS site was just being implemented along the way. It was something that should have been planned right from the get-go. The course was being offered via videoconferencing and the students were wondering "why do we need that (a website) right now?" But I did see the potential and I agree that it is useful. They (students) are used to Web sites but, with the platform, they had problems with passwords, access, etc."

On email: "In the beginning, I found it annoying. But, as a result (of receiving so much), I became more disciplined (in answering email) and told them that I would respond to e-mail at set times, like once every 24 hours, or during my virtual office hour every week. If I saw that I kept getting the same questions, I would bring them up with my students during the videoconference session. If my course was offered on the Web, I would do things differently, maybe with a forum or something."

On videoconferencing technology: "I kept having technical problems. They added some new sites, even one that was audio only. And the room was set up in such a way that I had to lean my head forward, towards the screen and (as a result) I often had a sore back after class. The image was blurry too. I think I would be better off not having any at all. Even the sound wasn't always good. For me, seeing someone's face is not all that important. Good sound and on-screen sharing, however, are. What I want is clarity. I use NetMeeting quite often (for screen-sharing). I told my students about it and some of my colleagues too. For student support, it is definitely a good thing."

On the effect the HCS has had on her course planning: "This is the most important thing I got out of the whole process. I realized that planning a course one week at a time was reassuring. It makes your job easier in the end. And the students are reassured. They know what is expected of them and they know what they have to do to meet those expectations. When are we going to do this? When do I have to hand in that? They know ahead of time what they have to do. The mood in the group is very positive. Fewer of my students wonder what they have to do and for when (and fewer of them ask me). It's like a contract, it's so clear. We agree on things together. We read it together and if there are things that need to be changed, we change them. Whatever we agree on stays that way for the term. I read it with my students and I return to it often during class, each week in fact. When you give a course for the first time, it's different. When you have given it several times, you are capable of seeing what works and what doesn't. So if either party sees something that doesn't work along the way, it can be fixed.

And the more detailed a syllabus is, the easier it is to come to an agreement with students. You put more time into it in the beginning but a lot less afterwards whereas right now, the course I am giving with a colleague has to be planned out each week.

At the end of the term, we see how things went and make the necessary adjustments. With the traditional course syllabus, where very few activities are actually identified each week, I tend to forget what we've done. As a result, I don't get to reinvest any observations I may have during the course in my course planning. Unless you take note of everything as you go along, which I never manage to do, you are better off doing more planning at the beginning."

On the future and implications for the design of higher education: "Planning is necessary if we want to encourage students to learn. There is a direct and palpable effect. Spontaneity is okay, but with current expectations among colleagues and students and with the little time available (for planning), people want to have an idea upfront as to what is going to happen in class. It is fine to go off on an 'adventure' (when teaching), but planning the adventure and being able to see the signposts along the way is even better. Systematic planning requires a method. A method is composed of several steps. Each step requires time and means. With conditions the way they are now, there isn't enough time to plan one's teaching properly."

Case Characteristics

The professor in Case 5 (see Table 10) had some characteristics in common with that of Case 4. Our fifth professor was female (F), at midpoint in her teaching career (M) and participating in the design of her course for organisational reasons (O). Also, the time between the beginning of our working sessions and the beginning of her course was short—the course was about to begin (1). Moreover, she had no experience with teaching at a distance (1). There were, however, two differences with earlier professors: she had some knowledge of instructional design (2) and had already defined her general objectives and a few specific ones (3).

Table 10: Characteristics of the subject matter expert

Gender	Rank	Reason	Time	Availability	No. of sessions	K/ Design	K/ DE	GO/ SO
F	ASC	0	1	1	4	2	1	3

Gender: female

Rank: ASC = midpoint (5-15)

Reason: O = organisational

Time-to-delivery: 1 = having already begun or is about to begin

Availability: 1 = 1 to 15 hours

Number of sessions = 4

Knowledge of Design: 2 = intermediate level

Knowledge of DE: 1 = no experience with DE

General Obj. /Specific Obj.:
   3 = GOs + SOs (SOs in limited number)

Finally, a pattern was starting to emerge. Was this a prelude to systematisation? —A sign of things to come? As usual, before our first meeting, I asked the professor to send me a copy of her course syllabus in its current state. She had a syllabus in the form of a "learner portfolio" which fairly well developed. It outlined, in some detail, how the course was to unfold. I also gave her the address of my website where I had updated my tutorials on "congruency" and "method" and I asked her to have a look at them to get an idea of the quickly-evolving instructional design model I was proposing. I also sent her a copy of the most recent version of the horizontal course syllabus (HCS) developed in Case 4. As with most of the previous cases, this course was about to begin when we met for the first time and the professor had been told by the department to prepare her course to teach it at a distance, like it or lump it! We therefore had to focus on the more problematic aspects of course design. Also, as a result of her limited availability, we didn't anticipate being able to meet more than four times.

Session 1: This working session began with a discussion of the tutorials. She told that me she had looked at them, that she had liked them and that, overall, she had understood the proposed design model. However, she felt she wouldn't have enough time to apply the model in its entirety and that worried her. To get going, we undertook a global analysis of her course syllabus, or rather, her learner portfolio. It was only the second time that I had ever seen such a well-developed document for an undergraduate-level course. In fact, it was much more than a course syllabus: it contained a general outline of the course, a list of course-internal policies, university regulations, resources, a list of guidelines for assignments, a methodology, a few examples of both faculty-centred and student-centred assessment instruments. Given the overall level of preparedness of her course and the time limit we were facing with regard to course delivery, we decided to focus on five main tasks:

1. Improve the quality of her lectures, particularly by developing a series of PowerPoint presentations containing graphics and figures to illustrate the numerous abstract concepts in her course. (This task was, in her opinion, the most important and would likely take up 80 percent of our time.)
2. Improve her course syllabus by creating a calendar for learning activities;
3. Check her GOs (general objectives), distribute them throughout her course on a weekly basis as well as complete and fine-tune her SOs (specific objectives);
4. In collaboration with the IDC (Instructional Development Coordinator), create an attractive, efficient, user-friendly yet basic Web site and transfer her didactic materials (as contained in her portfolio) to it;
5. Ensure that her assessment instruments were in line with her course objectives.

This is the first time that I have been able to work almost exclusively on one particular aspect of a course without having to worry about all of the other tasks that have to be done. In previous cases, I often felt that the "show must go on," even if our work on one week of the course was incomplete. I wonder if I'll ever get over that feeling. Maybe it is simply the nature of the beast—that a university course is ipso facto an incomplete entity which must constantly be improved, renewed and recreated.

Before focussing on her PowerPoint presentations, we started off our work by making a schedule of course activities according to the academic calendar for the upcoming term. Assuming a 15-week term, we determined that the actual number of working weeks would only be 12, by removing the following:

- the first week, which is normally devoted to the professor's presentation of the course syllabus and presentations by support staff (the IDC on learning tools and a librarian on accessing online resources);
- the midterm break week;
- the final week, devoted to exams.

Taking into consideration that actual coursework would cover a twelve-week period, we decided to divide her course into two, six-week units. During the first unit, the professor would lecture on the general themes of the course while assigning students both individual and team activities on a weekly basis. According to the professor's wishes, we then allocated the final six weeks in the course partly to in-class, student presentations to take place during the first half of the plenary session, and partly to subsequent group discussions, brainstorming and other interactive activities to take place during the second half of the plenary session. Dividing the course up in this manner provided us with a course structure based on thematic content areas according to which we could distribute the readings to be done each week. Having noticed a rather large amount of prescribed reading, I suggested to the professor that we go over each of the reading to determine how many pages she would expect students to read each week. As in Case 4, the professor decided to remove some of the readings she had seen were not essential, given the amount of time available to students to carry out their activities. After having resolved to review her readings for each week of the course, we agreed that this realignment of readings would best be done outside of our working sessions. By this point, we had an approximate idea of which reading would go where in the course syllabus, even though the actual distribution had not yet been finished. We saw that doing so would require some degree of realignment of her portfolio.

> In working with professors on redesigning their courses, I have noticed that they often decide to reduce the number of readings that they require from their students. They usually come to this conclusion because, when using the HCS, they must identify their objectives, link them to content and then link content to specific learning activities. As a result, they often realize that they are being too demanding and that, in fact, they run the risk of students simply refusing to do the required readings, especially if no points are awarded for it. Points cannot, on the other hand, be awarded to everything unless the professor is ready to mark everything. Consequently, the importance of individual and team assignments becomes immediately apparent because, by directly linking the readings to course assignment activities, the former become a requirement to completing the latter, and only the latter need to be marked.

The task of selecting appropriate readings brought us to examine the distribution of her GOs. As mentioned, her GOs were bunched together in one area of her syllabus/portfolio, as is common practice. We also still had to finish writing her specific objectives. In her syllabus/portfolio document, she had provided a list of six general objectives but she had not indicated where, in her course (or even how, for that matter) her students could meet these objectives. After discussing the matter, we distributed her GOs throughout the course schedule, with some of the more salient general objectives appearing more than once throughout the weeks. When we finished the process, two new GOs emerged, which we added to the syllabus.

Now that we had a basic framework for her course, she wanted us to re-examine her readings to determine to what degree each one enabled students to progress towards the GOs. I decided that the best way to proceed was to let her tell me about each one of them and, in listening to her, I would try to mentally link them to her GOs and also start writing down some SOs (specific objectives). When she had finished explaining the importance of each text that she wanted her students to read for Week 2, I told her what I had written down (the SOs) and got her feedback. In doing so, I was able to figure out, in pedagogical terms, her intentions for her students that week. We proceeded in the same manner for Weeks 3, 4, and 5 so that I could give her a *modus operandi* for writing her SOs. For Week 5, she informed me that she should have no problem continuing this task outside of our working sessions.

The site: Now that we had a good number of items in hand (the somewhat revised course syllabus-portfolio and several texts in digital format), we sent them off to the IDC so that he could begin creating and populating her new website. I suggested that she also send a brief biography and a photo or short video, to post on her home page—a gesture that students usually appreciate. She agreed. The IDC also said he would put her in contact with the technical support team's photographer/videographer so that he could take a picture (or make a clip) of her in her office.

Session 2: *PowerPoint Presentations*: At this point, and at the professor's request, we tackled her PowerPoint presentations. Having already seen mine, she told me how impressed she was at how I had visually depicted the various concepts I introduced. Since she also had a number of abstract concepts, she believed they would be easier to understand if we could put them into a similar visual form of some kind, either representational, analogical or arbitrary (Reiber, 1994).[1]

We began working on her Week 2 presentation which introduced the basic concepts of the course. At the very beginning of her presentation, she wanted to show slides with definitions of each concept, but she had not had the time to look them up in the dictionary and type them out. I suggested she consult the *Office québécois de la langue française*'s free online dictionary at http://www.granddictionnaire.com. She typed in a word to obtain its definition right away, then copied and pasted it directly into her slide (citing the source). In a matter of minutes, she had included several definitions into her presentation. She was as pleased as punch! We then started to think of ways in which we could graphically depict these concepts. I asked her to tell me about the first concept, the main one. I asked her to explain its importance to me, why she felt her students had to master it, its nuances, characteristics, and as she spoke, I started drawing.[2] We then brainstormed together so that we could improve it.

My schematisation for her concepts consisted of presenting several basic geometric forms, each concept being in a different colour. Each form contains an extract from an interview verbatim and then, in the following slide, it moves to the background as a second form of another colour with its own text appears in the foreground. This was an attempt to represent the notion that there are various forces at work in any given situation, all acting in their own particular way, yet co-existing to represent the situation as a whole. At the end of the exercise, all forms appear together as a set, revealing a complex state of affairs, rich yet diverse.

After having proceeded in the same manner for subsequent concepts, we completed the slide presentation and sent it off to the IDC, who would hand it to the graphic designer who would then, working with our basic strategy, add a professional touch and send it back to us for sign-off. After that, the IDC would place the PPT on the professor's Web site.

Session 3: The second slide presentation we tackled was the introductory one planned for Week 1. She had wanted to make sure that the Week 2 presentation was "in the bag" before looking at any of the others. In the first week, she wanted to present various fundamental concepts related to both the course material and to how the course was to unfold. As she explained these concepts to me, I sketched out some rough diagrams. In light of what she was telling me, I recognized that a systems view would be appropriate, so I drew a series of overlapping concentric circles. These would illustrate the relationships between each of the concepts in question and allow students to understand notions of intersection, shared experiential fields and views, reciprocal influences, and so on. We also explored the option of showing the students other concepts related to the systems approach, such as "open/closed systems," "natural/artificial/hybrid systems," "input/output," etc. She was quite pleased with our work but, rather than send it to the IDC immediately, she wanted to mull it over and make a decision about it later in the week.

When we had finished this part of the work, she told me that she was very happy with this way of doing things. She had long believed in the power of visualisation for learning and had always wanted to make graphic representations to complement her oral explanations but she had simply never had the time. She was very grateful to have my support in finally doing so; indeed, she told me that this was the first time she had been given the opportunity to work in tandem with anyone on the pedagogical development aspect of a course.

We then discussed her student performance assessment instruments and how to visually present each of them, showing how she intended to distribute course points to each one. She told me that she intended to assess performance in terms of four types of activities, namely:

1. in-class participation in discussions during plenary sessions;
2. an individual midterm assignment based on course readings (to be submitted as a report);
3. a group presentation (during a plenary session);
4. an individual end-of-term assignment based on an introspective and reflexive analysis of "my learning" during the course (to be submitted as a report).

I immediately pictured a timeline for the complete fifteen weeks of class, indicating the cut-off dates for each assignment. With regard to student in-class participation, we decided that it would probably be best (i.e. most equitable) were it assessed on a per class basis. This discussion brought up the question of how she would actually go about assessing class participation. The professor had decided that she wanted to award points for participation and not only for "end-products" (the assignments). However, she had only a vague idea of how to proceed. In the past, she was in the habit of taking attendance even though it was not compulsory, but she could not award points on such a basis since she agreed with me that attendance was hardly an accurate measure of learning (but it helps... Woody Allen was fond of saying "90 per cent of success is just showing up!"). Nonetheless, she was intent on finding a way to assess student participation. It was now up to us to find out how.

Assessing class participation is a difficult thing to do. How do you assess it? In the normative manner as in comparisons among students? X intervenes more often than Y? Or in a criteria-based manner but according to what

criteria? Everyone must participate...number of student interventions?
X number of times? Even if what they have to say is not relevant to the
discussion? I don't think so. I wracked my brain for various assessment
strategies I had seen in the literature and the idea of the "reading grid" came
to mind: as the student was doing his/her reading, they would complete
an analytical grid with which they had been provided. Granted, it is not a
direct way of measuring in-class participation. However, it was indicative
of preparation for participation, and it had the benefit of being an activity
which, if carried out correctly by the student, would likely have a direct
and positive effect on participation. For how can a student participate
intelligently in a discussion if he or she has not done the necessary readings?
By assessing a student's preparation for class, would that not put professors
on firmer ground to more accurately assess the quality and relevance of
each student's participation? If so, this would mean that individual or even
team reading grids would need to be developed. I could already hear the
professor groaning, "more work." On the other hand, it reminded me of the
old Québecois saying, "No money, no candy."

Session 4: During this working session, I broached the question of how
to distribute points, how the importance of each of the activities planned
would be weighted, the reasons for awarding points as well as how many
for each activity. I shared my idea of developing reading grids which could
be used to determine who was truly preparing for the course and who
was not. I explained that I was basing my reasoning on the fact that, in
order to be able to assess something, one must have both criteria and
instruments.

This discussion also brought to mind the idea that it is harder to assess,
and award points to, a process than it is to a product unless the process
has clearly-defined assessment criteria and known performance indicators.
I have found that faculty are often forced to assess what they cannot
measure. However, it seems clear, at least to me, that the accuracy of an
assessed result is inferior to that of a measured result. But this begs the
question: "Can everything be measured?" Another problem with measuring
is the question: "Are we measuring what is truly important?" and an even
more fundamental question, "What is most important?"

The professor agreed with the idea of developing reading grids because she had realized that her students had difficulty with several of the compulsory texts when she had to spend considerable time explaining the authors' perspectives. She liked the idea of providing grids to guide them through their readings in theory, but, as I had anticipated, she was rather reluctant to devote the time required to developing them. In the end, she agreed to take a crack at it, using her first text as a model. We got right down to it and we started reading the article together. As we read, I asked her questions and she told me whether they were important or not. Those she deemed most important were noted immediately. Since she knew her texts very well, in less than an hour, we had written our first grid. She now saw the advantage of the reading grid system and seemed ready to continue writing grids for the other compulsory readings in the course. To complete the whole process, she decided to adopt the *Socratic* approach, which is based on questions and answers during plenary sessions. To sum up the approach we adopted,

- she would only ask questions to those students who had submitted files to her, questions which she expected them to be able to answer without looking at their notes. Consequently, students who had not completed and sent back the grids would not be able to participate in the discussion or be awarded participation points,
- if she noticed that the students to whom she asked questions did not know the answers, she could decide not to award them participation points either.

In this way, she would be able to assess both a product (the completed grid) and a process (oral participation of students during the plenary session), both of which were closely linked to reaching her course objectives, particularly in terms of acquired knowledge assimilation and accommodation (Block, 1982).

It has become clear to me that a designer sometimes has to consider processes and products, the assessment of the former often depending on the measurement of the latter. I also realize that my background in measurement and assessment leaves something to be desired. I really must get in touch with a specialist in these fields so that I am better equipped to advise professors in terms of the various options available to them.

This case ended somewhat abruptly, sadly. The professor was simply "flat out of time" and we left off with some feelings of regret, knowing that we could have accomplished much more if we had just had more time. Below are excerpts from an interview I conducted *ex post facto*, where she reveals more about her personal philosophy learning which, I feel, is both rich and well balanced.

Ex Post Facto interview

On creating teams: "For the first activity, I leave it up to them, that is, they can team up or not. Then for the second activity, I create teams in random fashion (i.e. 1-2-3-4-1-2-3-4...) and then after that, for the term project, they choose their team members, to get a more 'natural' grouping. I have always valued teamwork."

On how teams function: "Teams function according to what you might call 'self-governance.' They can choose to form teams of between 2 to 4 members and carry out their work however they want, provided the end-product represents both the team as a whole as well as each and every individual in the team. Each student in the team should be able to see themselves in what is produced. The goal of all of my activities is for them to get other viewpoints on a given subject. In teams, they have access to just that."

On virtual teams: "They get together over the phone or by email and team presentations are delivered from different (videoconference) sites."

On the link between individual activities, team activities and plenary sessions: "The first time I had ever done anything like that was in developing my course with you."

On writing objectives: "At first, I was 'allergic' to objectives. Working with you forced me to develop them a bit more, but this had a pernicious effect as well...the students knew how things were going to unfold so well that they would freeze up, there was no more spontaneity...we had killed the element of surprise!"

On the course syllabus: "They (the students) had the full syllabus. They could see everything that was going to happen. Normally, I don't give them the course syllabus right at the beginning (of the course). Rather, I reveal it bit by bit. The students really appreciated the portfolio that we had developed further using the horizontal course syllabus. [...]... my teaching style involves their doing research on the 'inside' (internalizing) and then, afterwards, research on the 'outside' (externalizing), that is, reading what various authors have written on a subject. [...] I find that when I provide them with too many details or when I want to do something which focuses specifically on their personal experience, it is as though they lose focus, they get too concerned with details. Students find things much clearer when I use visuals (graphics)...I still use them today."

On her philosophy of education: "Learning is always a social phenomenon, you are never alone. Sometimes you try to read into the minds of others, sometimes you go out on your own, alone with your thoughts...We are the fruit of our experience...The very fact that we exist in an environment, in a society, means that we are never alone. We are always connected. If I walk alone, I am still part of a couple, of a community, of all that is living. We can reflect by ourselves but the minute we make contact with others, our reflections become anchored in reality. We define ourselves through others. Sometimes we are of two minds, two opposing opinions, like when we are not sure about something...Others do not stop me from being myself. Even Robinson Crusoe wasn't alone. I feel the most alone, in fact, when I am working with technology. I felt alone because, being naturally very independent, I get a feeling of dependency, a feeling of solitude...I really felt it when I went to see my students at their sites. I had felt some tension among my students when I was teaching at a distance but that wasn't enough to convince me that there was any. Because I was at a distance, I couldn't feel the effects of my teaching. But when I visited their sites, I realized how accurate my impressions at a distance had been. When I came back, I realized that my perception was right. I could feel what they [the students] were feeling."

On assignments: "I usually give them a term project with several parts, with all the parts related to each other of course."

On the design process: "It was a bit hard for me. We started our work before the strike and we finished after the strike. I was giving a distance course for the first time. I was happy that I was going to have someone to look at my pedagogy with me. What I remember about you is that you didn't want to change what I was doing. First of all, you sought to understand my method and then how you could help me reach my objectives. You are the person that I have talked to the most about my teaching since I arrived here [at the university]. I have been here for more than three years. At the start, I was afraid of what you were going to tell me, but that didn't last. You have a talent for turning ideas into images. I talked to you about my teaching and felt as though I was actually teaching you something. I had the feeling that we were doing something together."

On student passivity and teaching at a distance: "We still have a lot of discussions in spite of the distance involved. My on-campus students were the most passive. They were the ones who seemed to have the most difficulty coming to grips with it [the hybrid model of teaching]. I believe they were telling me that I was more 'connected' to the remote-classroom students, more in tune with their needs. In the second course, those on campus appeared to be struggling. They seemed to be saying 'we could have had a real course' while those at a distance seemed to be saying 'good thing we have this, otherwise we wouldn't have any course at all.'"

On the link between assignments: "Preparation is carried out individually and there is a team assignment. I give students a case study-based problem; they read it individually and reflect upon it so that they can then talk about it to their team. During the plenary session, we share reflections and identify problem areas...we pool thoughts and ideas. My goal is to get students and teams to develop their own views and to have them prepare a debate for the plenary session. And since each team works on a different problem, everyone participates in the debate. The idea is to show them that everyone can participate, that everyone has their own ideas."

Notes

1. This categorisation is based on work by L. P. Reiber (1994).

2. To preserve the anonymity of the participants in this research project, I cannot present the schematisations produced during our working sessions. In Appendix A, however, I have added examples of various graphic representations that I have developed from concepts linked to various domains under other circumstances.

CASE STUDY 6
I Did It My Way

Case Characteristics

The profile of the professor in Case 6 was quite different from that of the other cases (see Table 11). For instance, it was the first time that I had been involved in a case of this type. The professor was well into his career and had considerable time available for our work on the design process. In addition, unlike most of the others, he had previously taught at a distance. Despite these differences, there were also some similarities. This professor, like the others, had a minimal knowledge of the instructional design process. Although he was an experienced professor who, throughout his career, had developed a significant number of courses for institutions around the world, he had never developed a course in conjunction with an ID, nor in coordination with a technical support team. From the very beginning of our sessions, the professor expressed misgivings and was decidedly cautious (his guard was definitely up). Like his peers, he too had to design his course for organisational reasons. Also important was the fact that his course would be offered overseas.

Table 11: Characteristics of the subject matter expert

Gender	Rank	Reason	Time	Availability	No. of sessions	K/ Design	K/ DE	GO/ SO
M	FP	0	2	3	8+	2	2	1

Gender: male
Rank: FP = full professor
Reason: O = organisational
Time-to-delivery: 2 = beginning in 2 to 4 months
Availability: 3 = 31 to 45 hours

Number of sessions = 8+
Knowledge of Design 2 = intermediate level
Knowledge of DE: 2 = already offered one
or two courses at a distance
General Obj. /Specific Obj.: 1 = no objectives

Although some of these characteristics might normally be considered advantageous to course design and development, once again, a familiar scenario seemed to be emerging: we only had a few months ahead of us to get the work done. This time constraint, which has become a constant organisational feature (as in "plague") since the beginning of this study, created difficult conditions for proper course design.

Before our first meeting, I asked the professor, as usual, to send me a copy of his current course syllabus. Against my better judgement, I also gave him the address of my website where I had posted the tutorials on congruency and method and asked him to take a look at them to get an idea of the instructional design model that I was proposing. I also sent him a copy of the most recent version of the horizontal course syllabus (HCS) grid that I developed while working on Case 4 and improved during Case 5. When we met for the first time, the course was not about to begin. We had approximately a six-month time frame within which to work. This was more than I had originally thought we'd have. As a result, I eagerly looked forward to the possibility of carrying out our work at a relatively normal pace. But it was not too much time.

After talking with the IDC (Instructional Development Coordinator) assigned to the course, we decided to meet with the professor to explain our respective roles. I knew that the design (and development) process is relatively new for most professors and, consequently, they are unaware of what they can expect in terms of technical support. In addition, I considered our meeting to be important, especially at the outset of this process, as it would give both the IDC and me the opportunity to listen to the professor talk about his course, his objectives, and so on, and to start the process off with a mutual understanding of what lies ahead. Finally, sensing a degree of disillusionment in the team (especially among the IDCs) with regard to understanding the big picture, i.e. the complete design process from initial analysis to actual course delivery, I also wanted the IDC assigned to this course to feel more involved in the process from the get-go.

Sometimes, IDCs with little actual university experience do not understand the kind of didactic documents that most professors produce or even the nature of the tasks that they will be called upon to coordinate. As a result, sometimes they can be disappointed by the relatively simplistic nature of the production work to be carried out. While the project administrator may have informed professors that they would have access to leading-edge multimedia production technology, many of these professors still seek to use their websites merely as a "download centre" (or, "dump site") for digitized documents. This is because, in the minds of most professors (especially in the Humanities), didactic materials are still primarily texts their students are expected to read. Some have ideas about various visual representations they would like to have the technical team produce but these professors are in the minority. Most professors use visual means sparsely in their teaching and, as a result, the media aspect of their course has little immediate effect on the kind of work IDCs and the technical team actually produce. Only after faculty grasp the technological possibilities can they start thinking in such terms. And this is something which usually takes some time.

During my work in previous cases, I gradually came to see the importance of having the IDC present during my first meeting with the professor. Up until now, I got IDCs involved in the process only when the initial design work was over (there was always, of course, the feedback loop after the fact, which required redesigning some items). As a result, as mentioned, some IDCs, given the lengthy design process and depending on how many courses were stacked up waiting to be designed, experienced times when there was little to do. As developers, they were in between design and delivery and, as such, I believe they sometimes felt as though they were simply there to fill a purely technical, almost mechanical, role and didn't realize the high degree of creativity inherent in their jobs. The whole issue of teamwork (or a lack thereof) in an environment where such was not the custom, I observed, was turning out to be more and more awkward, even complicated, as we moved forward in the process. All kinds of jealousies, hurt feelings and suspicions of power-tripping seemed to be lurking just below the surface of our daily exchanges.

At this point, we had a change in overall Project Manager (PM). A former IDC took over as PM and this seemed to cause the axis of our project to shift away from what I felt was the centre (course design) and turn increasingly towards the end product (course production). In other words, it had moved away from matters of process and moved towards matters of product. The result was that overall project policy and, consequently, resources were increasingly being focussed on outcomes rather than on processes, which affected my access to resources previously devoted essentially to design. I found this unacceptable. Design necessarily precedes production, does it not? The architect must first do his work before the construction foreman comes on the scene. When such a power shift occurs, from design to production, an executive mindset takes over; executives tend to want to explain to the planners what to plan and how to design, but without any design expertise. As a result, their instructions/orders cannot be followed. Viewed in military terms, it was as though the tacticians start telling the strategists what to do (like a captain on the front lines who is seeing only *part of the action getting the authority to start dictating to a general how to run the war). This does not mean that strategists do not need input from tacticians, that is, those who are on the front lines every day. They do, and very much so. However, this input must flow up through an organisational hierarchy; nothing is served by turning the whole hierarchy upside down. The end result is predictable: miffed feelings, heels dug in, bad blood plus low design and even production values. The Résistance, however, is organising behind the lines...*

Session 1: The first working session took place in my office, with the professor and the IDC who had been assigned to the course. After the usual introductions, both the IDC and I explained our respective roles in the project. The professor asked a series of questions regarding the support he could expect to receive and the IDC, jumping in with both feet as it were, spent some time (a bit too much in my opinion) elaborating on technical aspects and production technologies, which appeared to have a soporific effect on the professor. I managed to bring the conversation back to discussing the immediate tasks at hand, the instructional approach I was proposing and fundamental differences between classroom-based courses and distance education courses. I asked him if he had looked at the tutorials (on congruency and method) and while he told me that he had, he did not seem the least bit interested in discussing their contents.

I realized that he may have had a look at them but that he had certainly not viewed them in their entirety. I got the clear impression that he had not understood them either. Whatever the case, it was obvious that he did not consider the contents to be of any importance. In my view, the contents pertained directly to the method that the university had decided would be used for the design/development/delivery of his course. For this reason, I felt it important for us to come to an understanding on how our work together should proceed. I decided that, from this point on, I would simply start each working session by showing professors the contents (congruency and method). That way we would all be able to get off on the same footing.

All of a sudden, hearing the IDC mention a pilot project that we had just begun (a synchronous-mode, virtual classroom software solution for course delivery[1]), the professor became keen to discuss the subject of course delivery (apparently wanting to avoid any further talk of design at all costs). He brought the discussion back to the IDC and asked about the delivery means available for his course. As it was going to be delivered overseas, he was interested in knowing more about using the synchronous-based platform, now that site-to-site videoconferencing was no longer a viable option (given funding and technical limitations at the receiving end). A long discussion ensued on the advantages and disadvantages of this type of instructional medium. The IDC, not having any experience using it for teaching purposes, began talking about how the software worked, its technical requirements, and so on, subjects which, in my view, were premature at this point. So I tried to steer the discussion back to course design. Using certain elements from the method, I tried explaining (and also to the IDC who seemed to have forgotten about them) the steps in the design process which necessarily *precede* those of development and delivery.

> *As I did so, I understood that the professor was much keener on the technical side of things. He had almost reached the age of retirement and did not seem interested in listening to someone 20+ years his junior talk about pedagogy (or, andragogy). He was also an early adopter of technology and seemed to be thinking he'd seen it all before. According to informal feedback from my ID colleagues, his attitude is common in the early adopter population segment. Few professors seem willing to listen attentively to an educational sciences specialist who is there to offer advice on instructional methods. The result is that IDs have limited room to manoeuvre and, consequently, often find themselves having to justify, even fight for, what they are proposing. Of course, this does not foster a very positive working environment. Nonetheless, I forge on...actually, it was more like trudging ahead...*

The professor went on to make some flattering comments about the design aspect of the method; however, they were obviously artificial and he could barely hide his interest in more delivery-related issues. The IDC, having finally found a spark of interest in what must have seemed to be a "dark night of the soul" in the project, got caught up in it all and kept the focus unwaveringly on delivery.

We still hadn't discussed what the professor was going to be teaching or how he was going to be teaching it yet we were already discussing how he was going to deliver it... now there's a dilemma for an ID if I ever saw one!

I finally managed to bring the discussion back to the professor's current course syllabus which was, of course, a very typical, vertically-arrayed, one-page presentation outlining thirteen weeks of course content distributed among thirteen themes. That was it! With the "analysis" step of the ADDIE model firmly in mind, I asked him if he knew about the other courses in the program and if he had ever looked at any of his colleagues' course syllabi. The professor answered that he had a pretty good idea of what the other courses were about but seemed somewhat miffed by my question. I went on to explain. We then agreed to meet again later in the week to carry out a global analysis of his course and locate its position with respect to the other courses in the program to be developed for distance education.

After perusing his syllabus, I saw that the professor was using the same compulsory textbook as another professor in the same program. Apparently, none of the students had ever pointed this out to them and, having never seen each other's course syllabus, they were unaware of the other's course contents and resources. Unwittingly, they were allowing their students to have what I'd call a "free ride." I am just now realising that this is the second time I've seen this phenomenon during this project.

I'm also realising that it is not a good idea to invite an IDC to the kick-off working session with a professor. From what I've seen, the IDC puts the proverbial cart before the horse and, for that reason, I was unable to get the professor to focus on design, i.e. getting him to start looking at his instructional strategies and activities with regard to his resources. Course delivery of a finished product is the final step in the process and talking about it prematurely only serves to deviate from, or perhaps more appropriately, derail our train of thought!

Session 2: This time, the professor has brought all of his course materials with him. The diachronic analysis I intended to undertake with him would allow us to properly position his course with respect to the other courses in the program, that is, if the professor was ready and willing to do so... I had my doubts.

I believe that an ID's first task is to make sure that course objectives are clear and distinctive with regard to other courses in a program, both with regard to courses offered concurrently, a priori or a posteriori. This positioning task of each course within a given program is typically undertaken by a Programs Committee when a program is launched. However, over time, I have noticed that a certain degree of what I term "course drift" may occur because of new currents in ongoing course development as undertaken by new faculty, as older faculty retire. As a result, the actual position of individual courses tends to shift around. I think of the global analysis phase in the design process as I do the functioning of a GPS: it is used to determine a course's objective position and relative position within a given program at a given time. However, carrying out this task properly and to its full and logical conclusion takes time, time which the professor in question was definitely not willing to lose, understandably so. Consequently, I had to be content with a cursory look at the other course syllabi which were just as underdeveloped as his. I noticed two things:

1) From what I have observed, program development in higher education is at times a relatively murky process and far from being systematic, especially when you compare the process as it naturally occurs in traditional universities as opposed to, for instance, its occurrence in distance education universities. The approach that I advocate, however, is systematic and hence the cause of constant conflict between myself as an ID and faculty. The result is this: I am forced to adopt an approach which is less systematic than I had initially hoped for and less in conformity with the most fundamental principles of ID. I have to adopt an approach which is more "hand-crafted" than "manufactured," an approach which reacts to both the desires and objections of professors. (Mamma mia!)

2) Issues of power and influence in the professor-ID working relationship are never far below the surface. Intellectually speaking, professors accept the "ID concept," although when it comes to actual practice, they refuse it. Since the university has guaranteed the teaching profession absolute control over their courses, the ID can only serve as a mere advisor to them. The result is this: even technical-pedagogical decisions fall within their jurisdiction. The ID is thus relatively limited in his ability to carry out the design process in a rigorous, systematic manner.

Consequently, the end-product of design will necessarily be a compromise between how much professors are willing to contribute (i.e. in terms of time and effort) and what the ID considers as a bottom-line. Once again, I observed that an instructional design model such as that proposed by Dick and Carey is not at all applicable in the university context because time, i.e. adequate time for design is simply not available. And it likely never will be.

We completed the analysis of the other course syllabi and were ready to begin using the horizontal course syllabus (HCS) grid to design his course. At this point, the professor asked me to explain, once again, the means of course delivery available to him. Obviously, he was interested in talking about any other subject than design. I briefly answered his questions and tried to bring him back to discussing his course syllabus, which we then slowly proceeded to examine. His typical practice was to provide readings to his students (in the form of a photocopied compilation) which they were to study before coming back into class. This discussion of his course material appeared to interest him and, since it could potentially open up the door to our discussing design matters, I seized upon it and we then began looking at his texts. (I decided not to talk about objectives for the time being as I intuitively knew it would be a touchy subject.)

I asked him about how he divided up his readings from week to week, since a distribution pattern did not appear in the syllabus. He told me that he would typically inform students, one week at a time, which readings were to be done but he said he had never actually taken note of the exact sequence. I explained that, in distance teaching, having more structure (I avoided the term "order") had proven to be beneficial, especially in light of his wish to minimise e-mail traffic and telephone exchanges between plenary sessions. There was a price to pay, however, for this expedience: his expectations and requirements would have to be specified in his course syllabus. Sequencing readings according to a course outline would mean that we would have to redefine his syllabus in terms of weekly themes and assignments. From a first glance, it appeared that he had a significant number of texts for some themes and only a few for others. Was this imbalance due to certain themes having more importance than others or simply because he simply had more material available to cover them? We looked over his themes again and identified the course's sub-themes, which allowed us to delve deeper and deeper into the very heart of his course. As he spoke to me about the linkage between themes, I discretely started taking note of the specific objectives that emerged. I intended to discuss this with him later on. For the moment however, we focussed on identifying and sequencing the themes and sub-themes, as well as associating readings with each.

I asked him about how he covered the readings in class. He told me that the readings provided students with the basic concepts of a given theme and that he elaborated on them during the plenary session by way of lecturing but mostly by on-the-spot questioning (using the Socratic question and answer method). He said that he relished putting students on the spot, that it was good for their minds. I asked him if he had any personal notes on his presentations and he did have some rough notes and key sentences that he kept in a notebook but he emphasized that his classes were largely spontaneous events, as were the questions he asked his students. Being extremely familiar with his readings, indeed, having written some of them himself, questions came to him automatically. He also explained that his follow-up questions varied according to the answers he got from students. If he detected an error in a student's logic or a lack of understanding of a given concept, he would reformulate the question and then ask another student to determine whether the error was unique to a given student, whether it was in his wording or whether it was a commonly-shared misconception. If, indeed, it turned out to be shared, he would go back over the topic in question and clarify matters. If it was an individual problem, he would usually just tell the student where he or she could find the appropriate information on the subject and then move on with his presentation.

This approach seems quite typical in higher education, at least in certain faculties, and is considered to be, quite rightly in my opinion, a major strength of the on-campus university teaching tradition: the withering interrogation followed by the exaltation of getting it right or the shame of publicly going down in flames, only to arise again from one's own ashes during the next class. The challenge is this: how to reproduce, or simulate this in distance teaching? In thinking this issue over, I recognized the importance, once again, of the role of dialogue in the construction and sharing of knowledge. Socio-constructivists claim that knowledge acquisition must go through the crucial stage of negotiated meaning. Knowledge does not exist in and by itself, but only the mental representation that one makes of it. What a student cannot represent mentally will never truly become acquired knowledge. An environment which encourages the negotiation of meaning is one in which students can converse openly and directly with both their professors and among themselves. If the classroom model is the ideal model, and if the on-campus classroom is to be simulated, then the classroom in virtual space must be recreated in a way that offers the same dialogue and information sharing possibilities. This is exactly what we were hoping the virtual classroom (the synchronous platform with which we are experimenting) would be able to do.

Predictably, the professor returned to the issue of course delivery, so we began talking about the synchronous platform and the results the team had been getting. Up to this point, none of the professors had used it in their teaching, and only some of them had participated in tests using it, mostly because of the agreement that had been reached between the Continuing Education Service, our corporate sponsor/videoconferencing service provider and its client groups, essentially requiring that all courses be delivered via videoconferencing (VC). However, as mentioned at the outset of this case, videoconferencing was simply not an option for the delivery of this course since the students were located abroad and did not have the technological infrastructure needed to access VC. Consequently, our discussions centered on how to use the synchronous platform, its functions and available tools. Given this overriding concern the professor had for course delivery, I asked the technical support team to set up a time for testing the platform with the receiving institution overseas, which I hoped would take place before our next working session.

Session 3: Since our last session, a series of technical tests between the receiving institution technical support team and our team had indeed been carried out but they met with only mitigated success. The platform we were using could technically and potentially allow hundreds of users online simultaneously, overall server speed and bandwidth permitting. Our team informed us of severe technical constraints at the receiving site in their lack of bandwidth. As a result, the receiving institution would be forced to limit logins to one user at a time and have his/her monitor projected onto a large screen in a classroom. They planned to have a technician seated at the computer workstation, who would manage discussions by having a cordless microphone passed around the classroom, thereby allowing students to participate in turns. However, from a pedagogical standpoint, I felt the virtual classroom, not unlike a regular classroom, was optimally designed for about twenty-five students entering and using the site at any one time, with each student working from an individual work station.

An academic meeting with the program head of the receiving institution had been set for today. The professor came to my office and I logged on at the agreed-upon time, establishing contact with the program head some fourteen time zones away. After the usual introductions, I intervened briefly on the instructional possibilities of the synchronous platform software we were using. I discussed the educational value of the various system tools with the professor and his colleague and we all shared ideas on student and faculty needs as well as the system's technical requirements with respect to the institution's resources and limits. This arrangement would, in theory, enable a group of students to participate in a live (real-time) discussion with the professor.

However, despite our having limited the connection to one lone user at the receiving site, the connection speed was woefully slow and it considerably affected our ability to interact. At this point, the professor started to lose enthusiasm for the whole undertaking. He claimed that, although an avid fan of innovation and relatively experienced with ICT, he did not like the lag in discussions over the fourteen time zones we were spanning. He anticipated that this delay would be overly disruptive in his class activities and would be an impediment to his pedagogy. I wholly agreed with him and, towards the end of the meeting, we all agreed that the connection speed at the receiving site would have to be substantially improved before we could even consider the possibility of using this platform for his course delivery.

After the end of our meeting with the foreign program head, the professor and I started thinking about other technical means that would minimise his dependence on the synchronous platform but would still allow him to deliver his course in a suitable manner and according to his expectations. I talked about various tools he could use to develop and deliver didactic material in a unidirectional manner and in asynchronous mode via the Web platform. I showed him an example of a course which I had recently completed with another professor. It basically consisted of a website that was relatively well-appointed with numerous readings and various documents such as sound-enhanced PowerPoint presentations as well as pictures, diagrams, tables and figures. It also had an internal email and discussion forum. He said that, at this point, aside from some texts that would require our reaching an agreement with the publishers on intellectual property rights, he had few digital documents to post on his site. He had his book which students usually bought from the university bookstore and a compilation of photocopied course readings but virtually nothing in digital format. He gave me a copy of his compilation so I immediately handed it off to the IDC to could get started on making the appropriate arrangements with publishers about digitisation possibilities. He considered his list of readings not an exhaustive one and wanted to add a few articles to it, yet it was a good starting point for both us and the IDC.

As for didactic materials, I suggested the idea of individual and team exercises. He told me he had never designed exercises of this kind but was willing to try. I provided examples from other courses (all quite generic and without specific contents so as to protect the anonymity of the authors involved) and we started to consider the extent to which these exercises could be useful in his instruction. At this point, I showed him an adapted version of the "pyramid" analogy that I had used in other courses and which aimed at enabling students to construct their own knowledge base through individual and team work. I explained that individual assignments were meant to prepare students for team assignments (second-level activities), which in turn prepared them for plenary session activities, located at the very top of the pyramid. The contents of the assignments could pertain to the various information elements that the professor felt it was essential for his students to know, that is, he could essentially draw from the same questions he would ask his students orally in class. In this case, I proposed that he write a series of questions in advance—a mix of open-ended and closed-ended questions—and post them on his course website. I also proposed that he write a series of questions intended for teams, this time more open-ended, thought-provoking questions which would likely raise student critical thinking levels. Afterwards, I proposed that he start experimenting with the discussion forum and attempt to deliver part of his course in asynchronous mode. We could, however, attenuate somewhat the "asynchronousness" of the medium by his being online at the same time as his students, thereby being in a position to exchange messages with them and provide almost instantaneous feedback. I knew that, given his pedagogical style and penchant for direct verbal communication, this was not the ideal situation for him. However, I framed it as a temporary solution that would allow us to get the course off the ground so to speak, while we waited for a technical solution at the receiving end that would allow us to exploit the synchronous platform fully. He told me that he would try the forum out to see whether it would be possible for him to function in this manner.

Session 4: We began this session with the intent of writing an individual assignment (IA) and a team assignment (TA). We went through the professor's first text together. He identified the points which were important for the students to know and I highlighted them as we moved along. These highlights would allow me, firstly, to start writing up closed-ended questions for the IA but, secondly, and perhaps more importantly, to identify his true course objectives (which I continued to note, once again in a discrete manner). As we moved through his text, I asked for his feedback with regard to the questions I was writing and he adjusted the wording accordingly.

> *I feel as though there is often, in the minds of a lot of professors, a degree of confusion between writing questions based on a text (as with test items) and writing specific objectives. I often have to explain that specific objectives (or SOs) identify skills and knowledge, among other things, that will enable a student to understand a text's contents while questions target the information contained in the text. This difference rarely seems obvious to professors at first but after discussing it with them further, I am generally able to help them understand the difference between the two. In fact, I often hear professors say that, after writing up their SOs, they start noticing the same objectives (or very similar ones) popping up throughout their course. Now that is substantial food for thought...*

Using these more close-ended individual questions as a starting point, we then started writing up more open-ended questions intended for the team assignment (TA). This assignment consisted of a series of questions which were less factual in nature, more open to interpretation and thereby likely to encourage a range of different answers, hopefully even a debate among team members. These team questions were written according to a constructivist bent, meaning that students would be called upon to confront the opinions, interpretations and inferences of their peers. I thus established an assignment template of sorts for both types of assignments that the professor could replicate once it came time to write up assignments for his other texts. As a result of this rather laborious process, the professor realized that, if he wanted his students to truly understand the texts he asked them to read, he would have to eliminate some of them. This was because the method we were in the process of developing (IAs and TAs followed by a plenary session via an asynchronous discussion forum and, eventually, via synchronous desktop conferencing), while potentially beneficial to his students, was starting to appear to be prohibitively time-consuming.

We thus returned to his original course syllabus and thoroughly examined the series of readings intended for his students. He reworked his selection and changed the distribution sequence for the 13 weeks of classes. This brought us to the end of our working session. Before we went our separate ways, the professor told me that he would send me an IA and a TA for Week 2 of classes before our next session.

Session 5: Since our last session, the professor had sent me, as agreed, the IA and the TA for the second week of readings. Having had just enough time to look at them prior to our session, we began our work by studying them together. I had noticed that the professor tended to write very short, specific questions such as Who did that?, What is the term for this?, What year did this or that take place?, etc. In response, I suggested he develop his questions further to make them a bit harder, because his type of questions might lead students to simply exchange answers among themselves without making an effort to find answers on their own. Writing questions using qualifiers such as "in your own words," "drawing on your own experience" or "providing an example" would reduce this risk and require that the student devote individual effort to finding answers. Should the professor notice systematic similarities in his students' answers, he could let them know that he expected individual activities to be completed *individually*.

With regard to his TA, I noticed that his questions were, on the contrary, too wordy. His sentences were, at times, simply too long and certain portions of them, because of their complexity, lacked clarity. I pointed out a number of examples of questions that would require some revision. He appeared to agree with my observations.

> *Up to this point, his reactions have been quite reserved, as though he was sizing me up. I was also getting the feeling that, although he was seemingly interested in "entertaining" my input, I got the distinct feeling that I might be invading his territory, so to speak, by means of my comments, as though I were nonchalantly stepping on "sacred ground," one which none (especially mere mortals) had ever dared tread. I felt compelled to emphasize, once again, the fact that my suggestions had to do with writing up didactic materials from a strictly instructional standpoint, i.e. in terms of the mental models (Gentner & Stevens, 1983) his teachings inspired in his students, and that they had nothing to do with his academic content per se. He told me that although he had never worked with an ID before and that this approach was quite new to him, he was OK with the way things were going. Indeed, he confided in me, saying that he had never spoken to anyone (meaning his colleagues) about his course content, aside from his students. Consequently, he admitted that our working together was both a source of inspiration and insecurity for him. Once again, it struck me just how precarious the ID's situation is (professionally speaking). The ID may inadvertently barge into an area with the best intentions in the world only to have the door unexpectedly but firmly shut. His or her role is still a novelty, one which is generally not acknowledged in importance. I feel as though the ID is walking on egg shells every time he seeks to lift the veil on the professor-centered, traditional university course planning process, a highly individual process which seems to be rarely discussed, relatively obscure and even expressly hidden from other faculty members.*

With regard to the professor's TA, his questions tended to closely reproduce those in his IA, but more vague. I suggested he write TA questions that would require his students to pool the answers they wrote for their IA, thereby constructing meaning on a collective scale. In order to encourage his students to negotiate meaning, piece together elements and ultimately draw conclusions, his TA questions would need to be more open-ended. Consequently, we went back over his TA questions and, rewriting them as we went, we made sure we followed the same numbering scheme as that used in the IA. We then attacked the IA and TA for Week 3. This time however, for each question in the IA, we also immediately wrote a draft question for the TA. The latter questions required students to carry out certain tasks such as categorising answers obtained during the individual assignment, summarising them, analysing them in terms of specified criteria, etc. I explained the concept of metacognition (Flavell, 1979) and how it applied to what we were doing. The questions we were writing would require that students process, sort and/or piece together the knowledge they acquired.

I also suggested that he include diagrams with his texts. The goal of a diagram (or schematisation) is, I explained, simply to assist students in their understanding by providing them with a "starter" mental model. I outlined some of the research in the field of cognitive mapping, visualisation and mental constructs and, as a result, he expressed interest in developing diagrams to add to his readings and assignments. Two connected concepts in his field of study caught our attention: "continuity" and "rupture." The text we were working on dealt primarily with these two concepts but it was quite difficult. Quite spontaneously, I sketched a diagram on the spot. We talked about the visual aspect of the concept and we together worked on developing what I had drafted (see how this visual representation evolved in Appendix 2). After having drawn up four versions, we agreed to think the concept over a bit more and then ended the session.

Session 6: We began our session with another look at the diagrams, the last version of which we decided to keep. I sent it off to the IDC so that he could send it to the graphic artist. She would develop a more professional-looking version (probably using Illustrator and then Flash) and would get back to us with a prototype for our sign-off.

As we had done the last time, we began by working on the IA and the TA that he had written between sessions using the models that I had given him. I noticed that the professor had simplified his TA writing style, slightly, and that his sentences were easier to read. Nonetheless, IMHO, his style still tended to be quite wordy and his sentences were still too long. Consequently, the readability level was relatively low and even clearly unsatisfactory in places. We spent some time exploring other, simpler ways to write his questions. I suggested, for instance, that he ask one question at a time (some questions had several sub-questions), that he formulate questions that require a complete answer, rather than a simple yes or no, that he make questions more neutral (i.e. not containing any elements that appear in the answer or any elements which give the answer away), etc.

Although the professor had a wealth of experience and was a self-professed Socratic scholar, I have a hunch he had not developed the ability to communicate with his students. He seemed able to speak to them, but not actually commune with them. His explanations were far too fine-grained for undergraduate students and his sentence structure was generally too complex. I noticed two things:

1. *He wrote as he would when communicating with his colleagues, which was obviously not what was required here (we are far from Holmberg's (1983) "guided didactic conversation";*
2. *His speaking style was identical to his writing style, which was not appropriate for the current context.*

These observations of mine, which I believe I had put forward in a respectful manner, have nonetheless apparently been interpreted by him as my calling into question his pedagogy and, as a result, they were not at all to his liking. As the words parted my lips, it became clear that I had made a major faux pas (closely related to il ne faut pas). A cold north wind had just blown into the room. There are times when I wish, as Annie Lennox phrased it in the lyrics to the song "Why," that I had "just kept my big mouth shut." This was one of them. Diplomacy, I silently told myself, is an essential skill for a designer, an art acquired through experience, not something learned in the classroom. It is acquired over time, if one survives the learning curve...

Despite these headwinds, we continued on, reformulating his questions. As he listened, I gave him my explanations, reasons and arguments. (Talk about being in the hot seat.) We went through everything with a fine-toothed comb. He gave me the reasons for his phrasing and we proceeded in this way until the exercises were completed. We came out of the whole process with well-developed exercises which read quite nicely.

During this work session, we established our *modus operandi* for the coming weeks. He insisted that we continue working on the exercises, however in asynchronous mode. Since the professor was not always on campus and had limited availability, he proposed leaving a copy of his texts with me and emailing his exercises to me each week so that I could read them and give him my feedback. Afterwards, we would send the "finished products" to the IDC who, with the help of various members of the technical support team, would give them their final processing. One final round of feedback was planned should the professor or I find any processing errors. We also agreed to have interactive work sessions over the phone and using screen-sharing software to produce diagrams for various concepts in his course which were the most abstract and the most difficult for his students to grasp.

As we were ending the session, I asked him if he wouldn't mind identifying and working on parts of his course which were most problematic, that is, areas where students tended to struggle, obtaining the lowest marks, etc. I explained that the design process is all about identifying problems, finding solutions and developing the tools to facilitate the learning process. The professor didn't make any promises, but he told me that he would think about it.

> In my experience, every course has such "black holes." In most cases, these are areas which generally do not receive the attention they deserve. Students stumble and fall, likely because they are areas for which there are few didactic resources, i.e. exercises and activities which provide students with a walk-through. I tend to consider these areas a top priority because dealing with these problem areas can make all the difference to students striving to understand and get good marks.

Subsequent sessions: Over the weeks that followed, we continued to develop exercises directly linked to his readings. Particular care was taken to write clear instructions for his students on how the individual assignments (IAs) and team assignments (TAs) were to be completed. (A series of tests among a small representative focus group had revealed comprehension difficulties which prevented them from completing certain parts of the assignments.) The most work to be done concerned the team exercises, understandably so since the professor had no prior experience in writing them. We also found several websites which could be used as additional didactic resources for students. Unfortunately for unilingual French-speaking students, all of these sites (except for one) were in English, there being few French-language resources available online in his field. We included the URLs of these sites in the instructions for virtually every individual exercise. Some team exercises were also linked to these sites although the focus in the TAs was more about students pooling their IA results and then developing a synthesis of the concepts studied.

Over the course of these sessions, we brainstormed on ideas with the technical support team on how the plenary sessions could be held. They informed us that, after subsequent testing, they had essentially hit a brick wall. The receiving site could not, at the present time, boost their bandwidth for this course. It would be possible for the professor to talk to his students using the synchronous platform software but it would not be possible for students to answer him in real-time (due to the low bandwidth and time delay). Students would be able to answer him via the chat but their real-time participation would be limited to this intervention mode only. Together, we decided that the professor would proceed each week in the following manner:

- The professor would post a written overview of the main concepts covered in the didactic resources for that week on the course website and he would provide students with readings and an individual assignment for each week of classes;
- Students would complete the IA and submit it online. They would also work in teams and complete a TA before classes, choosing one team member to submit it;
- The professor would provide feedback asynchronously (via the website) on what he felt were strengths and weaknesses in response

to the IAs. He would also send them feedback on their results for the week's TA;

- During the plenary session, technology permitting, he would provide a summary of the week's assignments and would introduce, as an overview, the main concepts as present in the readings for the upcoming week, making sure to highlight the importance of these concepts in the field of study and their relationship to previously-introduced concepts in the course. Hopefully, this session would motivate students sufficiently so as to complete the assignments and thereby develop their critical thinking capability.

It was here that I comprehended the extent to which the professor's role could have changed course had there been sufficient connectivity. Instead of carrying out the traditional role of knowledge provider, he could have played the role of a knowledge leader who interacts with his students, who encourages them to persevere, who instils in them a desire to carry on, who stimulates their intellectual curiosity and who forces them to confront, head-on, artificial barriers between them and their own knowledge-building capability. He could have been a source of inspiration rather than just another source of information, a motivator rather than a provider. Alas, access to this promising, liberating technology is not yet universally available. In spite of it all, even though we were unable to take his teaching to this next ideal level, at least his distant students would be in contact with a foreign expert, an experience which would allow them to be exposed to international standards and also to dream of what will be possible, eventually. Indeed, I firmly believe that it is only a matter of time, perhaps mere months, before even the most far away students are finally within our synchronous reach.

This reflection led to yet another: distance education was no longer th e best term to describe what we were doing. Almost overnight, we had moved into the online learning paradigm. Necessity and opportunity had moved us beyond the requirements and limits of distance education and, thanks to new online synchronous technology; we had entered a new universe of possibilities.

Our working sessions ended after a period of about six months, a time during which time the professor had gone from the initial design stage to the final production stage of his course. Given the time limits within which we had to work and the extent to which the professor was available to devote himself to this work and despite a number of moments fraught with a degree of mistrust and incertitude, our work had gone rather well. Throughout the course design process, the professor and I had sent off documents to be mediatised to the IDC who then dispatched them to various members of the support team. As a final step, the professor and I, as the course "architects" reserved the right to a final stamp of approval before our "house" was opened up to the public.

Ex Post Facto Interview

On the design process: "Under the circumstances and after talking with others who had spent three months "getting their course into the grid," I found myself in a difficult situation, being faced with using the grid (the HCS). Basically, I had a course to prepare. I thought we had only three months to get everything done."

On the method of instruction: "I had a certain perception of my teaching method. My students seem to like it. After 20 or 25 years, a lot of them say they have not forgotten my course. So, when you proposed a method that involved using a synthesis-grid, under conditions which bespoke of urgency, and with my assertive, independent-minded personality, I simply had to abandon it. Having abandoned it, I went off and used a totally different one. And I finished the course. And the students are working and they seem to be doing alright." (In actual fact, the professor did develop most of his course to the "grid," despite his being aware of this fact. The only part of the grid he did not complete was the Objectives column. Despite this, given the way the AI and TA are designed, the professor's intentions are nevertheless quite clear.)"

On writing objectives: "I help students give birth to ideas. I don't need to write objectives anymore. I want to expand their minds. They come to my course so full of certainty, their minds bursting with assurance. Humans bear the stamp of certainty and it is so harmful to them. I have only one concern: to bring students to doubt what they know. I want them to doubt their knowledge and then relearn it in a different way. You asked me to write objectives. They are so deeply embedded in me.

The problems we face are infinitely varied. You start with the facts and then you have to use critical thinking to solve these problems. It's just like a car accident. There are witnesses, weather conditions, mitigating circumstances...there are thousands of factors! How does one learn to take in all the facts while retaining only what is relevant?"

On his students' method of learning: "What do I expect them to do? I expect them to find answers to problems in case studies that they have never seen before. Take three different cases for instance: people are mistreated, made to feel scared and thrown out of their homes on the street...what can be concluded from these cases? How are they linked? It is up to them to conclude that all these cases concern a lack of security, or more precisely, a reigning state of insecurity. One must draw conclusions, understand consequences, find links between them, etc. from seemingly disparate facts."

On his teaching method: "I provide them with 'facts' as they were understood at a given time, or should I say perceptions of reality. Facts, of course, don't even exist. The problem with objectivity is one that dwells permanently inside of us. I want them to be able to reach conclusions even in the murkiest of cases. What we do is not an exact science!"

On targeted learning skills: "My students will become professional wordsmiths. The entire endeavour is a process. That's what getting a university education is all about. It is the capacity of students to search for and to find what they are looking for by themselves, through the use of their intellectual faculties. It's essentially an inductive process. I guide them through a series of readings and, above all, through an interrogative process. I don't want them to rewrite the course (that I'm giving). (...) I give them a series of readings and try to get through all of them. I try to get them to make connections. Their answers are predictable; I know how their minds work. I try, little by little, to bring them to make connections on their own and to put things in context without their having to spend hours preparing everything."

On his teaching method: "I hear positive things about my course...I put them in a situation and get them to feel it. It's alright to do that but there is a danger. Whenever I have them role-play, they accept the fact that I want them to get a feel for a situation. However, they don't really "get" it completely. Stepping into the shoes of a 13th-century king is not that easy. It isn't easy for Europeans and even less easy for Canadians. And what about foreign students studying in the South Pacific? When I expose them to these unknowns, there is the risk that they will think as one does in the 21st century; this confuses the whole matter. Historical recontextualisation and role-playing doesn't work that well. On the other hand, what I did find remarkable, in terms of multimedia, was, despite all the talk about design on a grand scale, there is actually no agreement on what it means to educators, even less so to students. I have an overseas student who very kindly sent me pictures of her wedding, of her children, etc. This kind of exchange was extremely enriching and one that never would have happened in class. Why? Is it because of the Web? Well, the Web does enable people to share things that we would not in class."

On his teaching method (continued): "My method is inductive but also partly deductive. There are a certain number of things (readings for instance) that precede inductive reasoning. You have to be careful not to fall into "facilitative" deductive reasoning. When a case is presented, all the incontrovertible facts are presented. The inductive approach involves questioning what we read. It calls on a student's critical thinking capacity while the deductive approach silences it. The road ends there. We resort to deductive reasoning because it is 'safe'. On the other hand, the inductive approach allows professors to "cover" a mere tenth of what can be covered using the deductive approach, but at least there is quality in it. An intelligent person can learn anything that's taught to him, whereas the average student merely repeats things back like a parrot. The student doesn't really form any ideas on his own. My method makes provision for the reverse, that is, for going from deductive to inductive reasoning and from inductive to deductive. There is no fixed sequence."

On the design method used: "In terms of the method we used, we did our work together and then I continued with things on my own. Thanks to the method, we landed the contract in Europe. It is systematic, etc. The method is inductive in its approach. Europe is still living in the age of dictation."

On how the project unfolded: "I believe that what I did is very different from what the others did. I provide them (my students) with questions and case studies and then they read them. They have to discover things through deduction; I force them to make connections. Once they have made an observation, or a deduction, I then ask them to look for substance to support their arguments. There are no texts to tell them how to go about that. Through questioning, they choose a path and follow it. Using a form of Socratic dialogue, I help them come to conclusions by accessing various sources. Hints are there but it is up to students to find them. I provide only a few readings ahead of time, only a few elements here and there. They tell me: "We didn't learn anything!," "We have so many questions!"...and I tell them "you have learned how to get by on your own." I don't "cover material"; it is impossible. There are thousands of things that can be said. Everything is done through analysis and reasoning. If that were done in every single course, students would turn out to be very different people. That's what a university is all about. No parroting. My most interesting and esteemed colleagues have their materials all prepared before they go in front of their students...."

On his usual in-class instruction: "I usually project texts onto a screen and we analyse them together. I go back over the questions that were raised and together we find answers. There is no one, single answer."

On how his class unfolded at a distance: "We had planned out 15 weeks of activities. I didn't manage to finish everything however. The students were not able to do everything. Either they would send me their answers to the questions too late, not at all, or at different times. Also, some students would disappear for a while and then suddenly reappear online. You have to be lenient and flexible at a distance because communications are more fragile. You also have to plan for power outages and local conditions, especially abroad."

On communication via synchronous mode: "My experiences with the synchronous platform were catastrophic. I don't know why. The first time, out of the 3 hours available, we only were in contact for one hour. The second time, after the first hour, everything just stopped. The third time, there was nothing at all. This is a serious problem. Then there was the time zone-related problem, a 14-hour difference. It was difficult to manage. There are also several levels of authorisation for students abroad which makes matters even more complicated. Synchronous mode thus requires a great deal of availability. In passive mode (i.e. asynchronous mode), everything runs fine. If people attend regularly, things go well. The reaction time is acceptable."

On teaching and cultural differences: "In Europe, professors feed, while students "regurgitate." The deductive approach renders them passive learners. No one dares say anything off the wall or risks proposing a slightly different hypothesis... I always believed that in North America people were more inductive in their learning; however, the case [study] method is not very widespread. Documentary resources are there to support reflection... my objective is not to "cover" the book. My objective is to add to the book. But I am not saying that the two approaches are not complementary."

On lecturing: "I don't like lectures that are simply repeated over and over again. A young student told me: "a professor failed me because I couldn't repeat what he said word for word." The 'parrot system' doesn't work for everyone. I have seen graduate students who, faced with problems, were not able to solve them. They didn't have the slightest idea of how to proceed. Lectures are a means of hiding from questions... it's because of basic insecurity, the fear of not knowing how to answer them. A professor's sense of security, especially a young professor's, takes precedence over a student's learning possibilities."

More on teaching method: "Each course, I tell them (students): "Here are the questions for next week. Send me your answers." The following week, I put up an overhead and explain to them where the group, not individuals, went wrong. This is basically how my classes unfold:
- I ask Questions
- Students answer them
- I give them feedback
- I get feedback from them
- Discussion

Using various documents, they are required to complete everything through inductive reasoning. They must reflect on the concepts and question their thinking. Didactic material and methods for organizing their thinking are available, but in insufficient quantity and quality."

Notes

1. Our technical support team started running a pilot using Centra Symposium (Now Saba Centra).

CASE STUDY 7
LET'S SHAKE TO THAT!

Case Characteristics

This is the first case where the professor (M) got involved in the process for a personal (P) reason: "to leave it to posterity," in his own words (see Table 12). As a full professor (FP), he had substantial time available (4) and he met with me face-to-face at first, and then we collaborated asynchronously. Given the relatively high level of collaboration, I estimated our meetings at 8+. This was likely because he was on sabbatical leave for a year and the design of his course was a priority for him. He had not yet set a start-up date for the course (3). These latter elements created conditions that were optimal for course design. Finally, his previous course outline included a fair number of GOs and SOs, an excellent jumping-off point for redesigning his course.

Table 12: Characteristics of the subject matter expert

Gender	Rank	Reason	Time	Availability	No. of sessions	K/ Design	K/ DE	GO/ SO
M	FP	P	3	4	8	1	1	3

Gender: male

Profile: A = career advancement (16+)

Reason: P = personal

Time-to-delivery: 3 = over 4 months

Availability: 4 = more than 46 hours

Number of sessions = 8

Knowledge of Design: 1 = low level

Knowledge of DE:
    1 = has never offered distance courses

General Obj. /Specific Obj.:
    3 = GOs + SO (SO - limited number)

I had a discussion with the Instructional Development Coordinator (IDC) assigned to this course to explain my reasoning in terms of when (as in later) he should become involved in the current project. He informed me that the project leader had insisted on his being present at the first meeting. I said I would speak to the project leader on the matter. He said that he too would speak to the project leader. The tension was palpable. I did speak with "*el jefe*," giving him my reasons for not wanting the IDCs present during initial meetings with professors (i.e. their presence tended to distract the professor and impede the natural flow of the design process by focusing on the latter steps in the design process). He said he agreed with me and that the IDCs would be told to wait until the design began to emerge before getting involved in development.

> This was where I felt, yet again, just how limited the instructional designer's (ID) authority was in this whole process. If the ID is truly the project "architect," then the IDC or "foreman" wouldn't dare challenge his working method. But, in our case, the project leader (who would likely be the "homeowner") tends to treat the ID as he would one of the tradesmen, like the electrician. So, as ID, my reaction is basically knee-jerk: I I am gradually withdrawing my commitment to the project. But, just as the homeowner is not an architect, the project leader is not a design specialist. In our case, he is an administrator without any training in education, even less in design. It is starting to dawn on me that, throughout the process, from one course project to the next, the number of obstacles and downright hassles I have been encountering is increasing exponentially, namely interference by administrators and "subordinates" (here I mean the IDCs). I am beginning to get fed up. How will all this end?

Before our first meeting, I had asked the professor, as I normally do, to send me a copy of his course outline. That would be our starting point. However, contrary to my usual practice, I had not given him the website address where my tutorials on congruency and method were posted. Instead, I decided to present them to him and discuss them with him at our first meeting, since we had the luxury of time.

Session 1: At our first session, I introduced myself, described my role in the design process and told the professor that I had received his syllabus. I recalled the goals of his course and showed that I had grasped the essentials. Next, I simply asked him to talk to me about his course, how it fit within the program, etc. Thus the "global analysis" stage began. He explained that his course was the first one that the students were to take in their program. He told me they have French-language courses as well as other courses of their choosing, i.e. fundamental first-year courses. However, since they needed professional pre-requisites to be accepted into this program, the first weeks of the course focussed on a review of the requisite skills, to ensure an appropriate level of preparation for each student.

We looked at the course outline together. It was a vertical course outline, quite typical, divided into four parts:

- Course content (approximately a half-page), containing brief descriptions of the main content to be "learned" in the course;
- Assessment (about a quarter page), where the types of assignments were identified as well as the respective assessment levels that were required of students;
- Course materials section (about another quarter-page), containing a bibliography (he did not specify which of the books or articles were compulsory reading);
- Attendance (a half-page), where he clarified faculty policy on student absences from class, consequences, etc.

He had never broken down or divided up his content or objectives into weekly segments of the course, preferring instead to let himself be guided each year by the "level" of his students. When I ask him if the course objectives varied from year to year as a consequence, he said that, indeed, they did. In fact, he said he had never written down his objectives, since he felt they were implicit. He went on to explain that he tended to allude to them as his students gradually advanced through his course. It is at this point that I offered to show him the Horizontal Course Syllabus Model (HCSM) that I had used with previous faculty members who were also redesigning their courses. He agreed and during the next 90 minutes, I presented the Congruency Principle and ID Method tutorials interactively as well as the HCSM. Throughout, I answered his questions spontaneously. At the end of the presentations, I mentioned websites he could visit to review them in part or in total.

We continued with a summary analysis of the program's other course syllabi, and especially the next level course to his. Since the same professor also taught the next course, I observed that there was not a lot of overlap in his two courses. However, it was hard to be sure, given the fragmentary nature of his syllabi (as well as those of his colleagues).

Our session ended with a discussion about writing instructional objectives in order to have at least one general objective (GO) for each week of classes, ideally with a number of specific objectives (SOs). He agreed to take time to formulate his general objectives and to insert them into his syllabus. For instance, we began looking at themes that would be addressed during the second week of his course (the first week was focused on presenting his syllabus and on technical-logistical questions). We discussed his didactic intentions for Week 2 in general terms and, together, we wrote down a general objective (GO) that summarized what he intended to achieve that week with his students. Afterwards, we identified a few specific objectives (SOs) that naturally stemmed from the GO. We parted company with his intention of starting to identify his GOs for each week of his course. I provided him with a copy of Richard Prégent's *Charting your Course*, a book on course design with a great section on writing objectives.

By and large, I liked Richard Prégent's book very much, even if I did not agree with him on the matter of GO identification. He states that general objectives are to be written from the professor's point of view. I maintain that, on the contrary, all course objectives, whether general or specific, must target the student's acquisition of knowledge and, as a consequence, must be written from their point of view. I believe that Bloom (1984) supports this position since, when he speaks about levels of cognition, he focuses exclusively on the learner's acquisition of knowledge, comprehension, etc., but he certainly never mentions the professor's levels of cognition...

Session 2: The professor admits that he had difficulty continuing the objectives-writing assignment. He had formulated three general objectives for weeks 3, 4 and 5 of the course, but had not written any specific objectives.

His GOs include what I consider, as mentioned above, an error in objective-writing; that is, GOs are too often faculty-centered. I have relied on the following UNESCO-based resource and I encourage faculty to do so: http:// tinyurl.com/6f99up (since the URL was too long, I used the www.tinyurl,. com site to abbreviate it, thereby avoiding the danger of a broken link).

We discussed his GOs and rewrote them so that they were student-focused. We continued rewriting his GOs from one week to the next. As we advanced, the professor realized that he must decide on which themes and content he intends to cover each week. Since he had never done this kind of breakdown before, he found the task quite difficult. There was frequent moving back and forth and to and fro between weeks, setting aside certain themes and moving others up in the syllabus. In some cases, we discarded some of them because there were simply too many to develop into learning activities. I reminded him that instructional design was an iterative process, and that nothing was absolute or definitive in what we were doing at this moment. I reassured him that we would be constantly moving things around as we worked. As the identification of his general objectives tied in nicely with a more precise definition of his content, the professor seemed pleased with our progress. But, he also seemed to tire of writing objectives and wanted to complete content identification so as to begin designing assignments, because this aspect of his course was under-developed. Consequently, we continued to work on his content.

He usually provided resource materials to his students that were part of a compilation he photocopied for them every term. They were centered on "learning objects" (Wiley, 2002) that students were to read, analyze and then interpret in their own way. The very first objects included a demonstration model with examples of how to read and how to analyze samples. The course's ultimate goal was for the student to produce his or her own learning objects, as a result of studying the examples provided.

I use the term "object" because we are not dealing with text. In the context of this case study, I consider the term to be sufficient in describing the nature of the resource material. Naming it specifically might identify the professor, which could be detrimental to the confidentiality I have guaranteed to all the professors taking part in this study.

Since these objects include a coded language that the students must master, the very first models provided by the professor are designed in such a way that he is able to ascertain whether or not the students already know the language (indeed, they should know it, given the program's pre-requisites). These first "object-models" become, as a consequence, a sort of review for the students and the subsequent object-models progressively become part of new language elements that will raise his students' technical competency levels. Because the professor had mastered the language with ease and depth, it got to a point where I had to remind him that, as an ID, I was a novice in his field, and could not follow along. We needed to focus on *how* he was to transmit content so that the students could achieve the course objectives, rather than on *what* he was presenting. The conversation swung back to a more didactic level and we carried on, examining the type of assignment that he wanted to develop for his students.

I then shared with him the individual assignment and team assignment concepts. He admitted that all of his exercises up until now were destined for individual students, and that he had never thought of having them done in teams. I told him about the socio-constructivist approach in education, about the importance of working in teams, and he agreed to think about whether he might be able to write team assignments.

Although his collection of teaching objects was well put together and, for all intents and purposes, complete, I noticed that his method for doing exercises in class would need serious transformation before delivery via distance education. Normally, he presented an object-model and then produced another of similar type on a blackboard, asking his students to quickly read, describe and analyze it. Students then were required to submit their individual sheets (detached from their workbooks) at the end of the class. The professor would then correct them and return them to the students at the beginning of the next class. He wondered how he could maintain his pedagogical practice while teaching an online course.

Seeing that this type of task could likely be supported by software and that there was probably already a program out there to assist students in completing this kind of task, I asked him if he knew of anything suitable. He said he had never thought of it but that he would conduct an online search to see what was currently on the market. I told him that the IDC in charge of his course could also help him with his research. I explained further that his students could likely carry out this kind of work in a virtual classroom (by using real-time or synchronous mode technology) but it could just as well be done in asynchronous mode, outside of the classroom, either individually or in teams. That concerned him because someone other than the student registered for his course might complete the assignment. We discussed ways to prevent "cheating." I asked if there was only one way to read or analyze one of his objects and he replied that there were in fact hundreds of ways of doing so. I then asked if his students usually produced assignments that were exactly alike. Again, he said no, he had never seen exact copies; each student usually emphasized one element over another, etc. I then queried him on why this concerned him so, given that it had not been a problem. He recognized that he was probably just a little nervous about teaching at a distance. He concluded by saying that if indeed, some students did turn in identical copies, he would simply warn them about it. He then said that, after talking things out, he was satisfied with the approach we were developing and we finished the session on a positive note. Before leaving, I invited him to go back to writing his specific objectives (SO) for the subsequent course weeks to complete this part of the horizontal course syllabus. He agreed to try again.

Session 3: The professor informed me that he felt the *in extenso* development of his specific objectives constituted an investment in time that he was simply not prepared to make. He arrived at this conclusion thinking it would be best, in his case, to invest his time in creating objects and in developing his Individual and Team Assignments. Incidentally, he explained that the instructions he was going to give to his students at the start of each IA and TA would have clear and implicit objectives; that they would be part of the guidelines provided. I decided I would not insist. So we left SO writing for the moment and pursued our thoughts on creating IAs and TAs.

He announced that a software program actually existed that not only allowed his students to complete the tasks he wanted done, but that an instructor-version of the software also existed to help him create, edit and export his course materials. He tried a demo version and found it to satisfy his needs perfectly. Plus, the student software price was very affordable, not much more expensive than mass-market software, and his students would be able to continue using it in their second course next term. By ordering this software in bulk, there would be 15 percent off for his students. He gave me a demonstration and we were thrilled with this good news.

Since the implementation of this software pretty well changed everything in the course, we went back to the Week 2 IA and we started to rework it, importing new subject material and saving it in proprietary software format. It was easier to do than we had expected, because the software wholly integrated with the objects he had already developed via an import sub-program. Also, this software was able to copy-paste any textual annotation he wanted right over the object. We imported his first object template, added instructions and left enough space for the student to reply. The whole thing only took a few minutes.

Encouraged by this progress, we then started work on the Team Assignments (TAs). The professor explained that, up until now, he had always expected the students to do everything by themselves. He was finding that, when the students worked in teams, they had the habit of relying on one particular team-member and taking advantage of his or her work. This would always end up with varying levels of conflict within the teams, something he wanted to avoid. Consequently, we discussed the possibility of having them simply work in pairs.

According to Lee and Allen (2001), working in pairs is very effective in improving the quality of student learning. According to their study, this method is even more effective than working in teams.

The idea took root and the professor began reflecting on an appropriate type of exercise. I suggested an intermediate-level assessment between assignments, focusing on individual work to be completed by the students, with the synthesis to be done during the plenary sessions. I suggested an assignment that would leverage work already completed individually, such as peer evaluation. Once the student had completed the Individual Assignment (IA), he or she would send it to the professor and then share it with his or her peer. The TA could include a main activity, such as evaluating each other's IA and writing a critique of the other's work to highlight the strengths and weaknesses of the completed assignment. This sort of evaluation would be appropriate in this kind of course since the professor was especially targeting critical thinking for the students. (He had actually been wondering just how he could encourage critical thinking in this class.) So, I suggested that the student, upon reading his partner's critique, would also have a part of the Team Assignment to complete. He would react to the critique, justifying why he had chosen to answer the way he did, while also having the option of correcting his IA. The Team Assignment would then be sent off to the professor. We both agreed that this type of TA added significantly to the level of learning for his students working in dyads. As a consequence, we decided to continue writing his TAs using this model. The professor committed to continuing importing his objects into the software format and to creating the IAs and TAs for the next two weeks.

Session 4: We had now established a functional working protocol. He imported objects into the software format, he wrote out the IAs and TAs and we reviewed them together. He had decided, since our last session, to attribute points in his course exclusively to the Individual Assignment and Team Assignment output by his students.

Next, we decided to talk about the plenary session process. He told me that, now that his students would be completing the greater part of their work outside of the classroom, he wondered what was going to do in class. In fact, he was laughing as he saying this because this was the first time he had ever faced a problem like this; before thinking about teaching at a distance, there had never been enough time to answer all of his students' questions. He spent all of his time teaching in a professorial lecture format. He now understood that he had never really had enough time to be concerned with his whether or not his students were actually learning. He said that he was always too busy making sure he was "covering" all of his material. He went on to say that he was satisfied with the design process to date, that he was more and more aware of the importance of having students fully prepare for class by completing the assignments we were designing for them so that, when they come into class, they have already completed the preliminary work and have good questions to ask. He also said that he had been in the habit of presenting them everything "on a silver platter." Now he was happy to assume a more indirect role, being less directorial and proactive and letting his students assume responsibility for their own learning.

This professor's realization confirmed my working hypothesis which I'm sure I share with a lot of other online educators, i.e. the best method of learning, whether online or not, is when the student assumes responsibility for his own intellectual effort and where the professor guides, helps, stimulates, etc. It would therefore be important that the professor, after having provided all of the tools required to complete a task/assignment, not interfere directly in the content-learner relationship. Indeed, it is up to the individual learner to create his own working relationship (or dialogue) with the course content (learner-content dialogue), hearkening back to positions held by Wedemeyer (1979), Holmberg (1983) and Moore (1993). As a result, the student is in a stronger position, cognitively, to interact with his peers (learner-learner dialogue) and, subsequently, with his professor (learner-faculty dialogue). The learning triangle "content-learner-faculty" (Moore, 1993; Shale, 2002) is thereby balanced, allowing the learner to have recourse to various forms of support and supervision adapted to his learning needs and his own specific level of autonomy.

We now directed our discussion to the plenary session process. Based on decisions we had already made, his class resembled, schematically speaking, an hourglass (see Figure 7 below). For starters, he would review concepts seen during the preceding week, focussing on the weekly Individual Assignment but more specifically the Team Assignment, highlighting commonalities and differences in the work submitted, explaining mistakes made or particular difficulties encountered by the students. He would ask and answer questions and summarize the course content presented during the week. This discussion of work accomplished would then lead to a "link-up" with work to come the following week. At this critical junction, he would clearly explain the linkage between what they had been doing and what was now expected of them during the week to come. His double goal here was firstly, to provide students with an overview of what they would be studying and secondly, to stimulate their motivation and on-task perseverance levels. In between weekly classes, the students would complete their assignments individually and with peers (team) and prepare themselves for the next plenary session.

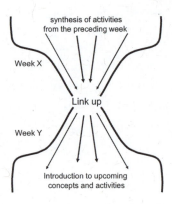

Figure 7: 'Hourglass' plenary session

The professor said he was pleased with his course's progress. Its new format was much more interactive than the original, and was, without a doubt, a better course. He told me he was especially satisfied with the way the plenary session would be delivered as he found it more organized and systematic than before. He also thought that his students would really appreciate this approach and he was looking forward to implementing it.

Subsequent sessions: The next sessions we undertook were asynchronous, mostly composed of exchanging documents with either my feedback or his, followed by didactic material references to be completed by the IDC. The prime reason for working asynchronously was that the professor was on sabbatical and out of the country for 6 months. From the moment he left, he continued to send me his IAs and TAs. I sometimes suggested reworking parts of them, but essentially the course was designed and would remain in this state until the next cycle of continuous improvement got underway.

Ex Post Facto Interview

On online courses: "It's too soon to tell where things are going. I think it looks promising but there is still a lot to do, a lot of technical things. I think there are still a lot of students who do not read the documents before class. It's not worse than before…there always will be some who don't."

On students: "For the better students, no problem. I think they like it… they can do it themselves…take this type of course] so it works well for those students, but I have quite a few who are completely lost. I don't think it's because the course is given electronically – they would be lost anyway because it's beyond their grasp – in their case, online learning does not help. It's a lack of preparation on their part. My first-year students are a very diverse group. I try to bring them all up to standard, but some of them have a long way to go. They're obviously all individual cases. One student is afraid of computers. She has never touched a computer in her whole life and is very dependent on her professors, on the course itself… in a case like that, any student would be lost. I get the impression that for those who want to dive right in, it's better for them, everything is there, and it's all well organized."

On plenary sessions: "No major change here, no time-saving... maybe I am the one who should change. Those who work well, who do their work, succeed very well. They are very good students. Some of them got 100 per cent on their exam. [...] I have three groups but the [Bell] curve is not like it used to be. There are a group of really good students, and then there is a group of really bad students. The results are polarized."

On teams: "I've been having problems with teams, but for different reasons. The stronger members of a team find that working in teams is a waste of time since the weaker members don't contribute much...they let the stronger ones lead. So I dissolved the teams and asked the students to reform them as they wished, and to just keep me in the loop. Some teams subsequently divided up the work instead of doing the activities all together. It seems they did not share results... they only divided up the work. But in the better teams, the work was undoubtedly done together and the stronger members learned the most because they had to explain the subject to the others. Therefore, with teams, I'm never sure what the outcome will be."

On weekly assignments: "While some are working, others go home on weekends, so they have problems reaching each other, etc. Even with dyads, it's no better. Keeping things balanced is hard. At the start of the course, I alternate between individual assignments and team assignments, but as we move forward, the workload increases and they have to do both individual and team assignments. Practice is very important in this course. It is not only cerebral; they must also acquire skills. They have to train themselves. And we, as professors, must train them so that they learn to work regularly and systematically. If they don't develop a method, they will not succeed. The theoretical parts are less demanding. They can get behind sometimes, but as for practice, consistency is extremely important."

On media-based courses: "I noticed that there are those who really want to work to their maximum potential. The online course allows them to work at their own pace. Everything is there for those who want it, but for the others, there isn't much you can do. If they don't want to work, they just don't want to."

On changes in the professor's workload: "It takes me twice as long to do my corrections. I print out the assignments, correct them and enter the corrections on the computer and then resend the assignments. Automatic correction is not viable because, in my field, there are simply too many subjective elements to correct. There is no one right answer. The accuracy of the answer depends on the manner in which it is presented. I might provide them with an answer key, which would shorten part of the correction work, but then, I don't want my answer keys circulating in emails. In class, I project the students' assignments, hide their name on the screen and review them."

On new subject: "During the plenary session, since they almost always have two types of exercises to do each week, I either emphasize one or the other. There is not enough time to go over everything. In order to get everything done that I want done, I must see them twice a week. When offered the chance to practice in the lab when I am there, they don't show up...they practice on the computers."

On multimedia and computers: "I am always learning. I thought of offering them the possibility of reach me online, outside of class times, but I haven't done that yet. Five out of fifteen of my students have bought the software to use at home, while others work in the lab. Some students appreciate this but most of them don't care much for technology."

On course sequencing: "I'm realizing that twelve weeks of subject matter is too much. If I miss a class, which often happens, I lose a week. If there is something I have learned through all this, it is to go through the syllabus in detail on a weekly basis, which I really like. There is no more guess work. I know where I'm going and I know where I'm at, [I know] what I haven't done yet... everything is planned. (...). There is a certain rigidity to it all, but I really like that everything is set up in advance... such and such a subject, such and such a week...from A to Z, no improvisation. But on the other hand, there's a lack of flexibility. I can't play catch-up. I do not want to skip over anything. The only way I have found is to reduce the activities to twelve weeks, with one free week."

On course planning: "In terms of planning, I certainly save time. Everything is planned. I study the material ahead of time. I check to see if the technical team has done its work, if everything is posted on my website, but I note that there are a lot of things to redo. When I work with the software… everything is fine, but some pictures are too large. On the other hand, if I try to reduce them [in size], things get blurred. So those that have been reduced need to be re-done to improve the quality. Now I put the pictures up myself, which reduces the support team's workload. In this way, I am satisfied with the quality."

On online tools: "I still haven't tried using screen-sharing software (SSS), nor the live platform. I would like to try to see if I would benefit. This could replace a plenary session in the classroom. And also, with SSS, I would like to see my students at work, see what they do to complete their work. Just like in a lab. Each student performs the experiment and the professor supervises. (…). I have not tried this yet, but plan to soon. At the end of the year, I want to try it. I wonder if, do I want to use on-line tools to replace the SP or for labs? I would really like to do the labs, work on individualization, but I don't have enough time. I want them to do more hands-on work. Time goes so quickly that we end up with lots of things unfinished. I would like them to make mistakes, start over and figures things out on their own. I would be there to help, to correct, but also to let them try to do it themselves. But, if I make time for this, I can't do everything else. Perhaps run some sequences that the students could view on-line, some case-studies, to see if they can go through the exercise, while they are hearing the professor comment on the student's technique. It could be a kind of on-line exercise, an added resource for the students who wish to use it…we could set up in advance and they could access it at any time. Then I could go into more detail."

On students: "They make so many mistakes. They invent things! The weaker students, for example, cannot distinguish between what's important and what is not. They depend on the instructor. Others can't grasp the way I present my subject matter. Some are afraid of computers, some refuse to even try. So, it's the multimedia aspect that separates them from the others. In other words, multimedia separates them from what they learn, which, in the past, was taught in a classroom in the traditional way. Must we cater to their needs or simply cast them aside?"

On moderating plenary sessions: "I am up-to-date in my course. No surprises there. My course is flowing relatively well. (Did you record what you said during your sessions?) No, I didn't think about recording my plenary session explanations... I could have put them on a site with visuals. This is giving me ideas but I am not quite there yet. It is true that I could add my comments to my learning objects...that would be an added resource for my students, especially when accompanied by a film or an animation. Otherwise, I have lots of other projects that are incredibly time-consuming."

On current projects: "I find the whole thing very interesting. It's all new, I love it! And it doesn't seem to bother students that I can always be reached. We move on, we improve; but the course will never be stand-alone; I will always be present. Quite simply put, the student wins out. The difference with a text book is that the resources [we've produced] are closer to reality. They can read and hear them whereas with a book, you can only read about it [the subject matter]. With multimedia, continuous learning can occur any time, even at home. It's about flexibility. And resources are more complete, closer to reality. A book is abstract, distant... multimedia reaches the senses. And there is diversity—it adapts to many different learning styles."

On the impact on the professor's workload: "It's more work, but this doesn't bother me. Corrections just take more time... (How do you shorten correction time?) That's the question. Automatic correction is difficult in my field. A justified interpretation is the norm and can vary a lot. Right now, downloading homework can take an incredible amount of time at home if one does not have high-speed internet connection. Especially since I always have students who are late handing in assignments...[it's usually] whenever they get around to it. Computers and humans are complicated."

CASE STUDY 8
MANAGING VOLUME

Case Characteristics

This professor's profile was similar to Cases 6 and 7 (Table 13). He was a full professor (FP) and was relatively available (3) which ended up meaning that we met more often than I had with the other professors (8+). He was personally motivated to proceed with his course design (P) and we had more time than usual before his course was to begin (3). Finally, his knowledge of design and teaching online was limited (1/1) and his current course syllabus contained only general objectives (2).

Table 13: Characteristics of the subject matter expert

Gender	Rank	Reason	Time	Availability	No. of sessions	K/ Design	K/ DE	GO/ SO
M	FP	P	3	3	8+	1	1	2

Gender: male

Profile: FP = advanced in his career (16+)

Reason: P = personal

Time-to-delivery: 3 = in over 4 months

Availability: 3 = 31 to 45 hours

Number of sessions = 8+

Knowledge of Design: 1 = novice level

Knowledge of DE/OL (online learning):

   1 = had never offered a course via DE or OL

General Obj. /Specific Obj.: 2 = GO only

Before our first meeting, I asked the professor, as I usually do, to send me a copy of his course syllabus as well as any program-related syllabi. Because this course was not about to begin and we had several months ahead of us (probably about six) to develop it, I actually started to breathe easier, as I had in Case 7. This time around, the allotted time was acceptable (although still minimal in any absolute sense).

Session 1: At our first meeting, I introduced myself and described my role. I demonstrated my awareness of the content his course syllabus by summarizing my initial analysis. I then asked him to tell me about his course content and of his interest in offering it online, etc. The professor was very enthusiastic about the possibilities offered by information and communication technologies (ICT), although he admitted he was not very familiar with their use. He had always taught in a traditional manner, and particularly enjoyed his weekly exchanges with his students. He says that it was one of the "joys" of being a professor. He also explained that his course was compulsory in the second year of the program. We looked at his current syllabus, a relatively well-designed vertical course plan but not very practical in terms of identifying which activities were to be completed in which week. I then presented him with the three short tutorials I had developed (in earlier cases). The last tutorial, on the Horizontal Course Syllabus Model (HCSM), really seemed to get his attention. He said that he found this model interesting because he had always wanted to improve his course structure but neither had the time to do it, nor a clear idea of just what to do. He felt that by linking all of the elements into one logical and coherent structure, his course syllabus would improve in clarity. As we left the meeting, we both resolved to undertake a parallel analysis of his current syllabus in light of the HCSM. We agreed that, at our next meeting, we would discuss transitioning from one to the other.

Session 2:   Since our last session, the professor realized that, by undertaking a critical analysis of his course syllabus with respect to transferring it into the HCSM, he was asking far too much from his students each week. He came to this conclusion when he was thinking about his weekly breakdown of activities and tasks that he expected his students to do. And yet, when he had originally planned his course, adding items as he went along, it had not seemed like there was that much work involved. At least, he said, he had not noticed. Now, after beginning to transition to the HCSM, he feared having to question maintaining some of his course content, given the quantity of work he now realised he was expecting from his students. So, we began this session with a critical analysis of his plan and broke down his content, one week at a time. This task generated the usual question: "Which objectives are linked to the content?" From this analysis, I intended to proceed to the design of his GOs and SOs.

As usual, we started with Week 2 of the course (the first course serving only to present his syllabus to his students and to give an overview of his subject matter). Aware of the fact that a lot of professors become frustrated when faced with having to identify their objectives, I did not insist. I got him to talk about his course and noted the GOs he wanted to focus on. I decided not to present him with my sample drafts right away, preferring to email them to him later. In this way, he would be able to re-read them between sessions.

Establishing general objectives connected automatically to the way a he had distributed his texts throughout the course. I tried suggesting he think in terms of his objectives *before* thinking about what reading materials he wanted to use because, I explained, one should first be certain about *what one wants done* before thinking about *what to use* to get it done. He had already used most of his texts in two other courses. (He just told me, in fact, that this particular course will be a blend of two other courses of his and that it would be less advanced and hence less demanding from his students than the other two because his students will be from outside his field.) He usually expected his students to read approximately 150 pages of text a week, including a chapter from his own book as well as several articles, a number of cases studies, a few technical reports and his course notes. Nevertheless, after my explaining the individual and team assignment concepts, he decided to decrease the number of readings to be done and to add more practical exercises, in the aim of enabling his students to apply what they were reading about. I took note of some potential specific objectives in Week 2, while he was explaining the themes that would be broached and the readings set for that week. Next, we considered the individual work for which students would be responsible. At this stage, the EM pointed out that, although he expected students to read about 75 to 100 pages of various articles and course notes every week, he had never before prepared exercises to facilitate their accomplishing this task. I mentioned to him that an individual assignment can serve as a guide or a kind of reading grid. I suggested we take the time to develop a model based on the key points in one of his proposed texts. The series of questions we developed only took about 20 minutes to prepare. I explained that the questions asked would orient the students toward the most important parts of the text. Moreover, these questions, aimed at the individual, also readily served as the basis for developing team assignments (TA).

In case the professor did not have enough time to do all of this, I thought I'd suggest that, especially towards the end of the course, he could have his students create their own assignment sheets and share them with their team members, a simple exercise to organise that would actually assist the students in better understanding the texts under study. In helping the students develop a reflexive analysis of the provided texts, the professor would also save time down the road by reviewing and including the best examples in future class material.

I shared this idea with the professor who was immediately interested. Because his instructional style draws upon the Socratic method—maieutics—(like the professor in Case 6), he took the position that it is extremely important for his students to develop their critical thinking by learning how to ask the right questions, i.e. to focus on the essential. To save time, he agreed that we should develop individual assignment models that his students could use to develop their own assignments. The professor could then devote more time to preparing his team assignments and weekly plenary sessions, which, in his opinion, would require a lot of preparation time. Now we started developing a few model individual assignments for the first weeks of the course. But, from Week 4 onwards, the professor figured his students would likely be able to write up individual assignments for the remaining weeks of his course.

Session 3: This week, we began work on the team assignments. This professor had never had his students work in teams or in pairs, so he was unsure of how to design these assignments. I showed him a few examples from other courses I had worked on and proposed a list of activities that could best be completed in teams or dyads, and we examined it (See Appendix 3). He saw that quite a few of the proposed activities would apply to his field but also pointed out that there were a few that he simply did not understand and still others where he saw no possible application. I answered his questions about potential activities for his course and gave examples of the unfamiliar ones. So we started planning his team assignment (TA) based on the activities he felt were most promising.

The first TA focussed directly on the Individual Assignment (IA) for Week 2, which required students to highlight the key points in two required readings that appeared to contradict each other. The open-ended questions of the assignment required students to compare their answers to individual activity questions and to negotiate any diverging opinions, in order to agree on their team answer. The team assignment provided a double-entry grid for synthesizing their answers. It was here that we realized that these assignments could best be done in dyads, rather than in triads or bigger teams. Consequently, the professor decided to create two-person teams, aware of the fact that this would require more assessment on his part but equally conscious of the benefit to his students. He wanted above all to create a quality learning environment. Moreover, given time constraints, he had the option of asking only some of the teams to present their results each week. However, everyone would have to be prepared, just in case...

The professor appears to be taking this design work seriously—a task he said he had never previously had, nor taken, the time to do. This is something I hear a lot since beginning these case studies. Professors want to plan their work in detail and their students' assignments but, because of the time factor, simply cannot manage to get it done or do it as well as they would like. They repeatedly tell me that having a designer to support them in this process reassures them and urges them to do their work thoroughly. All in all, the simple fact of having someone who values this work seems to release their energy. This manifest interest for the design work on their part thus bodes well for the future. It appears that professors who hear colleagues in their department, faculty or school speak about the work they are doing, are starting to introduce some of the said elements into their own courses.

We then moved along to the Week 3 team assignment. The professor decided that the texts for this week and the nature of the individual assignment lent themselves to a Web-research type of activity. He had already identified quite a number of interesting sites and Google-indexed them. As it had been some time since he had conducted this research, we went online and found two new sites that he felt were important. From these available-online resources, we studied the information that the students would be able to obtain and created a grid for them to fill out (showing categories with sample answers). The professor decided not to provide them with research parameters, descriptors or key-words. They were to discover these from the weekly readings. Now that the professor was confident in his ability to create Team Assignments, we decided that, at our next meeting, we'd focus on plenary session activities development.

Session 4: This professor was particularly preoccupied with the plenary sessions because he had always taught on campus in a traditional way. Hence, contact with the students was extremely important to him and he wanted specific details on the online "virtual classroom" environment. So I gave him a rough overview of the asynchronous learning management system (LMS) and the synchronous, virtual classroom platform we were using. (I also made a mental note-to-self to ask the project manager to meet with him later on and actually walk him through these tools, having him try them out). So I first showed him the functional capabilities of the asynchronous platform from the student's point of view.

> *I intentionally decided not go into the functional capabilities from the professor's point of view. Having already had the experience of seeing their eyes glaze over at how the LMS worked, or their being completely overwhelmed by "all that technology," I no longer wanted to chance their rejecting it out of hand. Accordingly, I started introducing them to the pedagogical features of the LMS, showing them how students could access their materials with the click of a mouse, 24/7. "Sell the sizzle" was the mantra playing in my mind. I would then leave them in the care of the IDC so that he would ease them into the editor-access mode. I saw that when I presented them familiar elements, such as accessing Word documents or PowerPoint presentations, etc., they were able to connect this to existing schemata, thereby better negotiating the transition from old to new. By collaborating closely afterwards with an educational consultant, they learn to become autonomous in getting their course online and keeping it maintained.*

I highlighted the advantages of the LMS: students had access-on demand; instructors could add or subtract content at will. In this course, the professor shared a well-known problem already mentioned by other professors, i.e. converting his numerous paper-based documents into digital format. The professors were constantly on a seesaw, on the one hand interested in obtaining free and unfettered access to knowledge for themselves and their students while, and on the other, concerned about protecting their copyright and that of their colleagues.

This dilemma is far from being resolved. For instance (at the time of publication), Canada's Access copyright agreement covers the distribution of photocopied documents but is silent on the handling of digitized documents, unless materials come under a Creative Commons license. Some faculty members maintain that what they write belongs entirely to them while others concede that their university may own a right to part of it or, at the very least, has a right to access what they produce. Still others, seemingly a minority, contend that university professors are paid to produce knowledge and that they receive all the support they require from their institutions to write and produce texts and thus disseminate their knowledge. Asking for further payment could denote a lack of professional ethics. Still others (perhaps an even smaller minority) even consider that requiring the students they teach to buy the books they have written is unethical, feeling that such material should by rights be digitized and placed online. These various positions reflect different levels of conflict of interest. The debate, though just beginning, will reach unknown heights in the years to come, to the point where the publishing industry might disappear, at least publishing houses as we know them today. To be continued...

Next, I presented the synchronous virtual classroom to him, again from the user/participant's point of view. I insisted on the fact that this environment would allow him to continue implementing his own pedagogy, thanks to the two-way communication software. One of his chief concerns had been how all of this would play out online. I emphasized that this software, besides enabling two-way audio communication, split-screen viewing, Web safari, application-sharing, and so on, was really not a lecture platform, but rather one for fostering problem-solving through dialogue. I also explained that his website, soon to be filled with documents, activities and resources, could better serve the purpose of lecturing because any kind of document could be uploaded there, such as Camtasia-enhanced (i.e. soundtrack-enabled), PowerPoint presentations. I told him that after putting all of your documents on the LMS (texts, Individual Assignments, Team Assignments, PowerPoint presentations with sound tracks, even video clips, etc.), you could lecture to your students and tell them everything you have to say about a given subject. And they could listen to your lecture when it best suited their schedule. Then, during the weekly online, real-time plenary sessions, your students would have their say. You would get a chance to listen to them report on what they had learned that week by working on the assignments (both Individual and Team). The synchronous platform gives them an opportunity to talk to you about what they have seen and understood. It is best implemented as a feedback tool. Afterwards, I proposed a series of tests with the synchronous platform. He seemed thrilled by the whole idea.

We then started looking at what the Week 1 plenary session would look like. The activities roll-out looked like this: first explain the technologies used in the course (backed up by one of the technical team members) and then move on to his course syllabus. In actual fact, these explanations would simply be a reminder because the students, upon enrolling in the course, would be automatically invited by email to take a tutorial on how the virtual classroom works, before the first session. After going through his syllabus (which would be up on the screen in PowerPoint format) and fielding the usual questions (usually on assessment details), he could then benefit from the platform's interactive components to conduct a "pre-test": a student survey to establish their degree of familiarity with course content. The idea here was to stimulate the students' imagination, to motivate them to stay in the course and to show why this course was a necessary part of their training.

Pleased that the Week 1 outline was sufficiently planned, we moved on to review the Individual and Team Assignments for Week 2. The professor, although a complete novice in online learning, had more than 20 years' experience in higher education, and he knew full well how to communicate with his students. Loyal to his teaching style, he intended to review the texts to be read and the exercises to be completed before each plenary session. I talked with him about my "hourglass" concept of how a plenary session might proceed (see Figure 7) and he immediately said "It's similar to what I have already been doing!" What interested him in this figure was that the procedure had been graphically represented. A lively discussion ensued on concepts emerging from his content that could easily be visualized. I proposed that we return to his plenary sessions because I wanted to make sure that he would be ready in time. He replied that, thanks to Figure 7, he now knew exactly what he needed to do. He said he was going to refer to the readings of the week by asking questions randomly, as he usually did, systematically focussing on some of the harder questions in the Individual Assignment and then moving on to the Team Assignment, picking teams at random to provide their answers. To conclude, he said he'd conduct a synthesis of the content studied during the week and then follow up with an introduction to what would be studied next week.

Ex Post Facto Interview

On the design process: "I found the process difficult in the beginning. I had to deal with two people, the IDC and you the designer. In fact, when we first started, we didn't know exactly who would be taking the course. The department head told me the course was for a group of foreign students enrolled in a regular program in our field of study. Once the design work was almost finished and about half of the production was done, I learned that the course wouldn't be for regular students; it was to be a more general course aimed at students from various programs. The course would be offered as part of a certificate program. So I discovered that the work that had done no longer fit the real needs because the clientele had changed along the way. But to top it off, the course methodology would have to change, meaning I could not use the Socratic method. In terms of student assessment, there would be no ongoing assessment but instead, one final exam worth 100 per cent; this I did not agree with. I refused to teach a course based on a method to which I did not adhere. Fundamentally, there was a complete lack of communication between the decision-makers and those who were producing the course. Control was lost when the design of the activities changed directions."

On the design model: "[Before starting,] I was aware of some of the design aspects. For instance, I was already using weekly readings and multiple-choice exams. So I had no trouble adapting to the [design] model. But the weekly 'breakdown' [into objectives, content and activities was something I had never done before but I was used to building weekly modules. What I liked best was the instructional method, the way of representing the subject matter and the data, and the way of simplifying it for those who are unfamiliar with the field of study, as is the case for first-year students. Incidentally, I used the method [sic] in my other courses. It is really interesting and useful. The results I'm getting are better. I find that the courses I've designed with you are much better built and much more planned out intellectually. The instructional objectives are clearer."

On the amount of course planning time required: "It took twice as long to set up this course than it took me the first time [I planned it]. Enough time to write a book! It did not take as much time [as it did the first time] to collect the resource materials. Breaking down the material into weeks is what took time. And defining objectives that are really targeted, developing corresponding activities, writing up quizzes, finding questions—providing students with the tools to understand the subject matter, the equivalent of twelve year-end exams, twelve times the explanations. I counted them all. Then I realized that I had done too much! If I had kept all of the exercises, there wouldn't have been a single student left in the course by Christmas. I had to remove some team activities because the students just weren't able to keep up."

On student assessment: "The closed-end [weekly] quizzes are corrected automatically but I asked a lot of opened-end questions which required a lot of correction. By not setting boundaries, students were free to submit their exercises whenever they felt like it – it was chaotic. Some got them in early, others late. A lot of discipline was required to succeed in a course like this one. On the one hand, if I let things be, they didn't finish the course. But, on the other hand, if I imposed a schedule, they dropped the course. I'm not sure where this is going. I always believed that this teaching method demanded a lot autonomy and discipline. It is not adapted to young students...it simply does not work. However, for civil servants, adult students, it's fine. So there is a problem with enrolments. There are a lot of requirements; we have a quality program but not enough enrolments."

On plenary sessions: "When testing the synchronous platform, some students participated in the trials. But others had problems in connecting. This type of teaching requires a lot of preparation; at least three hours of preparation for each course hour. The slides had to be sent to the technician twenty-four hours before the start of the course. I thought we could do a class] every week but we ended up meeting every two weeks, due to lack of attendance. It was optional. A lot of students couldn't get online, either because they had lost their password or for some other reason. The students did appreciate it but it required a lot of time and preparation [on my part]. You have to teach the course plus all the rest."

On supplementary work: "Slides need to be prepared because you can't have a student spend an hour and a half in front of an empty screen, it's just not possible. So, you have to show slides. We had some problems... forgetting to download slides, technical problems, etc. I created slides for the course material every week. But I'm always behind. If it's Week 8, I'm reviewing Week 7 material to summarize it."

On the workload: "It took a lot of time to prepare the slides. [This course] is the only thing I've done all year. I did not write a book, not an article... I can't do anything else. It's not normal. It's too much. And it's not finished yet!"

On how the course turned out: "It appears that the course we designed is not adapted to non-regular students – it's too demanding. But, fortunately, I can reuse everything we've done in my regular courses."

On interaction: "There's a problem with interaction. The students tend to not intervene freely. So I end up lecturing and they seem to like that. This lack of interaction is always the same, whether we're in class on campus or in virtual class online. Some have not done their readings. Their attitude seems to be: "we want the professor to summarize what we haven't taken the time to read." Especially among adults, this attitude is widespread. They're passive... bombarding them with questions is what's needed... I don't really know where I am at with all of this. They seem to like the course, the slides and presentations. We'll see what the evaluations say after the course."

On the software: "Another problem surfaced during course development. Regular students usually access an online website to consult the databases but the site owners insist that the [software] be used only by regular students. Since this course is aimed at non-regular students, this creates a new problem."

On results stemming from the design process: "The course is now much stronger, much better built. What's clear is, from an instructional point of view, I am very satisfied. I did not put my other projects aside for nothing. The documents produced are very interesting. It is very satisfying to see some beautiful visual presentations. Technically speaking, I want to be more autonomous...I am very independent. It is part of my profession."

On potential research: "[This design work] made me think more about communications, such as teaching seminars in my area of study. There is certainly a lot to think about."

On student autonomy: "What really astounded me was that one of my students is so enthusiastic about this online course [which promotes student autonomy] that he decided to enrol in the regular program."

On online learning and eye-to-eye contact: "One of the problems with distance education is that we don't know our students. In terms of communication, it is said that 90 per cent of it is non verbal.., but I can't see my students and they can't see me."

On instructional design: "On the whole, the subject matter is much more structured. If the student is not active during the [online] session, he is during the assignments [during the week]. I try to make sure that the didactic documents they have to read are closely linked to the concepts that I present in class."

On getting students engaged in dialogue: "Some have not read anything and don't know what to say, while others have read everything and understood nothing and have nothing to say; still others have read and understood everything, and so they have nothing to say."

On accessibility and autonomy: "Strictly from an accessibility point of view, these courses are accessible. In the past, students would never have been able to take these courses. It's an important victory, but it's not for everyone. One must be autonomous, and most young people lack the discipline to attend class and do these assignments every week."

CASE STUDY 9
I AND THOU

Case Characteristics

This professor's profile was different from the preceding case in that he was less advanced in his career (ASC) as well as the reason why he got involved in online learning: because of his department (O). But in contrast to many of his peers, he was actually very interested in experiencing the design, development and eventually the delivery of his course online. Like the professor in Case 7, he had a reasonable amount of time to devote to work on the design of his course (3). His course would not be offered online until the following year (3) We ended up meeting much more than most of the other professors, on a par with Cases 6 and 8 (8+). Like most of the others, he had never taught a distance education or online course and knew little about the design process (1/1). His course syllabus included general objectives, but not specific objectives (2).

Table 14: Characteristics of the subject matter expert

Gender	Rank	Reason	Time	Availability	No. of sessions	K/ Design	K/ DE	GO/ SO
M	ASC	O	3	3	8+	1	1	2

Gender: male

Rank: ASC = mid-career (5-15)

Reason: O = organizational

Time-to-delivery: 3 = in more than 4 months

Availability: 3 = 31 to 45 hours

Number of sessions = 8+

Knowledge of Design 1 = novice level

Knowledge of DE: 1 = had never offered a course via distance education

General Obj. /Specific Obj.: 2 = GO only

Before we met, I obtained a copy of his course syllabus. As in the two preceding cases, I decided to present the tutorials on congruency and design method during our first meeting. Once again, this course was not ready to begin immediately and we had at least six months ahead of us to design it.

The problem discussed earlier with regard to the IDCs getting involved at the start of a course project now appears, for all intents and purposes, to be settled. To avoid any further mishaps, I simply did not inform them of my meetings with faculty. The situation I had previously experienced with one of the IDCs that ended up getting the project leader involved confirmed my gut feeling that the IDC should only get involved in the process once the ID and the professor have had the time to actually design something, so that there is something to develop. Their getting mixed up in the design process simply makes matters more arduous (as if they weren't hard enough already...).

Session 1: At our first meeting, I introduced myself as usual, described my role and simply asked the professor to talk to me about his course. He explained that it was the follow-up course to one that I had previously worked on. So, this time, I knew exactly where his course was situated in the program. We thus moved along expediently, analyzing his general objectives and avoiding redundancy. Our analysis confirmed that his course had different objectives from the others. Only a few elements overlapped, at the end of the first course and at the beginning of this one, which we judged to be perfectly acceptable and even pedagogically necessary to demonstrate continuity. Even though the professor had already given this course several times, he now had to modify it to present it to a group of students with a different profile. He explained that he wanted to develop a *lighter version*.

This part (the analysis) went quite quickly since he knew exactly what he wanted to do, which types of knowledge he was targeting (mostly knowledge skills but also some metacognitive skills) and which general objectives he wanted his students to reach. The distribution of his general objectives (GO) throughout the course was, as is common, sorely missing. Moreover, he had not identified any specific objectives.

At this stage, I asked if I might present the model I had been using with other faculty for planning online courses and he accepted. I explained that many professors had already made use of this model and had generally obtained good results. I started by explaining the congruency principle. His reaction was enthusiastic and he was impressed by the simplicity and the clarity of the presentation. He also really liked the idea of using graphic animations of the more detailed concepts and wanted to try to design a few with me, because he had a lot of abstract concepts in his material.

I next presented the horizontal course syllabus (HCS), with the steps we would go through and why. Again, he said that my explanations enabled him to understand the direction in which we were moving but he voiced an underlying fear that the process would be overly ponderous. He was concerned that we would not have enough time to do everything. I outlined how I imagined we could build his HCS and that, in doing so, we could move through all of the design steps efficiently, ending up with an improved course that would likely produce foreseeable results. He said that, although he really liked the HCS idea in principle, he was still concerned with time limits, stating that he had heard from his colleague (in Case 8) that the amount of time it took to get a complete course syllabus done was *crazy!* I told him that we could start by simply transferring his current syllabus directly into the HCS grid and that, by working systematically, we would probably have it more or less completed in approximately three hours, that is, depending on what learning activities he already had designed and developed and depending on how well developed they were. I had to recognize that, were we to start from scratch, developing Individual Assignments and Team Assignments might indeed take a long time, even longer if we didn't get at it.

Session 2: We did...get at it. We divided up his GOs and distributed them throughout his course, adding some new ones on the way. His current syllabus was quite well defined in terms of content distribution as well as identifying the textual resources he intended to use. He had created, in fact, a compilation of texts (mostly from the public domain on the Web) and had set up a document format template for purposes of harmonizing text presentation. He would still be able to use it in his new, redesigned course but we both realized that he would likely have to reduce the number of required readings per week and maybe even add a few, easy-to-read "popularized" texts (mostly articles from general circulation newspapers and mass media) to take into account the non specialist characteristic of this new group of students.

Between the last case (Case 8) and this case, the technical support unit had decided, after complete testing had confirmed system robustness, to use the synchronous platform to disseminate part of the course and the asynchronous platform for distribution of course-related documents. Since the implementation of the synchronous and asynchronous platforms, the overall course delivery system was quickly taking form. The technical team even offered on-demand, pre-recorded technical coaching resources 24 hours a day, 7 days a week; they also offered individualized back-up for faculty by telephone or online chat during business hours plus extended evening hours (for night courses). I reminded the professor about the message from tech support that was supposed to have been sent out to all faculty and students who would be using both platforms. He appeared not to have noticed it in his email. I answered his questions as we moved along and told him he could have more intensive training on demand, as soon as he had more time, especially on the asynchronous platform which required about a day of training to learn how to use most of the course design features. In terms of the synchronous platform, I planned to have the IDC introduce it to him after we had made some headway on his course.

All of this talk about course delivery now had him wanting to discuss what his first course would be like. He admitted experiencing angst at getting started. I explained that the IDC would first train him in using the system. Then, on the day of his first class, the IDC would also demonstrate to students how the virtual classroom interface worked, especially how to use the microphone and emoticons to provide feedback to the professor. The IDC would also show his students how to access the asynchronous Web platform to retrieve course documents, use the forum, email, etc. Afterwards, he could then present his syllabus to his class, as he would in his on-campus classroom. He seemed satisfied.

We then returned to his course syllabus and to the HCS. We looked at week 2 and the professor told me how he usually got his course underway, by trying to activate students' prior learning from the first course of the program by focussing on the basic foundations of the field and by using a sort of interactive game of questions and answers that his students seemed to find motivating. Like one of his colleagues who taught another course in this same field, he frequently used the inductive approach to stimulate students' critical thinking. He wondered if the synchronous platform would be up to this spontaneous and quick type of exchange. I replied that he had to be aware of the momentary lag in communications required to open and close the microphone. I told him that, according to professional journals (like *EDUCAUSE*) which report on faculty use of new technology, it did seem to take some getting used to but that, after a few weeks, most faculty members tended to take it all in stride. However, only a trial run could convince him of that. Given his edginess over this, I wrote a note-to-self to request setting up the professor's account on the synchronous platform and to book an online session with the IDC as soon as possible.

We now started looking at how his course materials fit in his course to determine what exactly required redesigning. Just as in his on-campus course, he expected his students to do their weekly reading outside of class. He showed me the texts he intended to retain and which ones he would drop because of their difficulty, reminding me that this course, although compulsory for students in his own field, would now be open to students from any field, as an elective.

This session ended with the elimination of several texts. However, from the start, I had tried getting him to work on his general and specific objectives. I had hoped that we would be able to at least make a first pass through his course before finishing this session, but we had not. He then explained to me that he often worked from home and consequently was not often available for meetings on campus. I suggested that we try free screen-sharing software and showed him how it worked.

Session 3: Once we got connected online and I could see his screen, I suggested we begin this session by reviewing his general objectives, making sure they were evenly distributed throughout the twelve weeks of class. He managed to use the screen-sharing software without much difficulty and I followed his work on my screen, asking him questions while also making suggestions. It was of course a provisional distribution since general objectives often change places once we start writing specific objectives. As work proceeded, I asked him to talk about each week of class. As he did so, he granted me control of his screen and I began proposing various formulations for specific objectives. We assisted one another in correcting what we came up with and ended up with a list of specific objectives for Week 2. I suggested we continue working on Week 2, identifying at least one individual activity as well as the plenary session activities, before moving on to writing the specific objectives for the next week.

This strategy stems from an observation I have made during the course of this study. It is theoretically possible to either adopt a vertical strategy in formulating HCP components, i.e. develop all of the elements in one column, or adopt a horizontal strategy, i.e. complete all the elements in one row before moving on to the next row. I have tried out both and the horizontal strategy seems to give the best results. This was probably because professors exhibited greater satisfaction when they were able to close the loop on all the activities in a given week, before moving on to the next week. But when I asked them to design vertically, i.e. define all of the specific objectives for their course at one fell swoop, it just didn't happen. (I understand—if I were not a designer, I might also find the entire process unsustainable.) Consequently, I have adopted the horizontal strategy. After setting the specific objectives, I move along to the course content, then the individual activities, the team activities and finally, to the plenary session activities for that given week. I have also observed that the horizontal alignment of elements (in a given row) cannot begin until the general objective(s) for that week are identified. The winning strategy seems thus to be a combination of a horizontal strategy and a vertical one in that the process is initiated vertically; we provisionally define all of the general objectives for the course and then distribute them evenly, week by week, then continue on horizontally developing all of the elements in a given week.

With our cruising speed now firmly established, we succeeded in completing week 3 before the end of the session. The professor already had some individual activities planned but none for the team. I emphasized the pedagogical usefulness of team activities in online learning (i.e. they promote engagement and commitment) and we ended this session by exploring various types of team activities. We looked at the typology I had produced earlier (see Appendix 3) and he identified a few types that would likely suit his targeted course objectives. I also brought up the usefulness of his implementing a forum in the asynchronous platform and explained the difference between a *student-directed* forum and a *professor-directed* forum. He could choose either of course, depending on whether he had the time to get involved or not, or he could choose to limit his involvement. He liked the idea of creating a shared space in which his students would be free to discuss matters among themselves and was interested in participating from time to time. Then, after thinking about it, he said he was concerned that we would not be able to assume all of these new, online course-related tasks. He therefore felt he would be content with monitoring the progression of discussions in the forum without personally intervening. He was ready, however, to propose a weekly theme to be discussed and already had some excellent questions to initiate a debate, related to the cases studied during the week.

So, as, this session wound down, I resolved that, between now and our next session, I would ask the IDC to train the professor in using the synchronous platform to help him understand how the virtual classroom worked, thereby alleviating his worries. At the next meeting, we would also look at the steps involved in planning and preparing for his plenary sessions. In the meantime, we agreed that he was to continue to develop his objectives, course content and activities, using the HCS model.

Session 4: The professor had indeed been able to meet with the IDC and had tried out the synchronous platform. He said he felt it would perfectly suit his needs and those of his students who might be all over Europe and North America. Moreover, between sessions, he had devoted himself to his work and has produced complete versions of Weeks 4, 5 and 6. I was thrilled! We began reviewing his work and I noted that he had succeeded in developing his specific objectives (SO), in clearly identifying his content and in linking both to activities with great precision. I picked up on a weakness in his specific objective-writing, however. Rather than enunciate the specific objectives he expected his students to meet, he tended to simply draw up a series of tasks to be completed.

> I noticed that distinguishing between writing objectives and identifying tasks to be accomplished is a recurring difficulty among professors. Whereas an objective answers the question "what is to be done under what conditions and to what extent?" a task is simply how something that we define is to be done. I feel my chickens are coming home to roost… thus far, I have not required that professors write complete, Mager-based, three-component objectives because I recognize I would never get them. Instead, I have encouraged faculty to develop succinct action-verb statements, describing what they want students to achieve. In doing so, I now realize that I should spend more time helping professors differentiate between ends (objectives) and means (tasks). I also realize that I have to be careful to play my cards right. When I insist on details, I tend to "lose" the professors. I realize that design is one part science, one part art. The art of details! Everything is detail in this field, but if the ID is intrusive, if he or

she starts, as they say in Québec, "tripping over the flowers in the carpet" (I love that expression!), professors will just drop out of the process. We must therefore let some things go while insisting on what is most important. What is to be gained by doing so? Professors who finish the process! But what is lost? Pride in one's work as an ID. I'm always thinking: what if a fellow ID sees what we're doing? Might he or she say something like "This is NOT instructional design." In other words, one must not only choose one's battles, but also one's battlefields...

The difficulty this professor encountered (as well as all of the others) was determining how far he was to go in developing his specific objectives (SO), i.e. to the point of setting out everything, detailing everything? He feared that "telling all" would put limits on his teaching in two ways:

1) If something unexpected came up in his discussions with his students, there was a risk of his feeling cornered and unable to pursue it because it was not part of the planned objectives. I pointed out that planning objectives is important for that very reason: to avoid aimless wandering through perhaps interesting yet irrelevant "territory." Without set objectives, there was a constant risk of going beyond course limits.

2) By developing his syllabus according to the HCP, he was worried that he would be giving his students too much information on exam content. When I asked him for clarification, he replied that he wanted his students to prepare themselves for an exam without knowing exactly what would be on it. I asked him if this was justified. If he were asked, as a professional, to complete a task without specific parameters, would he agree? We had a good discussion and, in the end, he seemed less concerned about writing his specific objectives.

We then once again turned our attention to the plenary sessions (PS). He told me about his teaching style which was similar to that of his colleague in Case Study 8. I told him about the *architecture* of the plenary session (as defined in Cases 7 and 8) and he agreed with this type of course flow. Like his colleague, he very much valued dialogue with his students and informal discussion, but he agreed that the plenary sessions should be focused on answering students' questions rather than on his delivering content. He also acknowledged his tendency to want to dominate a discussion (not a completely unheard-of tendency among faculty...) but that he would like to modify this behaviour. I explained that, by establishing a set process up front, i.e. allowing student presentations, say via a team spokesperson, followed by on open-ended discussion, he could limit his interventions to a synthesis of weekly content at the beginning of class, answering questions mid-course and introducing upcoming content at the end of his class (in reference to Figure 7). Based on this simple protocol, we set out the following parameters for the plenary session:

- Plenary sessions would last two hours (as in Case 8).
- There would a 10-minute break after the first hour.
- Unlike the Case 8 plenary session protocol, this professor preferred to start with a content synthesis of the current week. This part should only take about twenty minutes of the first hour and, during the synthesis, the professor would use the survey tool to get a better sense of the students' opinions and conclusions about the concepts being addressed (an interactive session).
- The next forty minutes or so would be devoted entirely to presentations by individuals or by team spokespersons (depending on the number of students). They would present their conclusions on assignment questions.
- After the break, the professor would open up the debate on questions from the other students, for approximately forty minutes. He would act as moderator and answer any unresolved questions, in light of students' queries about the weekly assignment.
- Next, over the course of a few minutes, the professor would give a synthesis of the course content for that week.
- The last part of the class would consist of an overview of content for the following week. The professor would use this period to stimulate interest among his students for the issues to be addressed. He would explain how these issues are connected to subject matter previously seen. He would also briefly describe the upcoming weekly individual and-or team assignment.
- At the very end of the session, he would remain online for a few minutes (as he would in class on campus) in case anyone had

questions. He would also offer students the chance to ask him questions in the discussion forum, which he would answer during his *virtual* office hours (three hours a week).

The professor was quite pleased with this protocol. He could easily see himself carrying it out. Because it took into account his pedagogy, he was quite enthusiastic. We planned a meeting with the IDC during which we would try out the synchronous platform. I also enrolled the professor in a weekly, live, online exchange seminar I had recently started, in which faculty members who were interested in the new platform could become accustomed to using the learning environment interface, in both user and in moderator modes, at their own pace, in a non-threatening environment.

Subsequent sessions: Having by now established a *modus operandi* which functioned quite well, the professor began preparing one week of activities at a time, sometimes two, sending me everything at least 48 hours before our bi-monthly meeting in which we reviewed his work, shared our thoughts and arrived at an understanding. After each session, I met with the IDC and handed over what had to be produced or simply uploaded. The IDC would then send us any produced material for sign-off. At our bi-monthly meetings, we reviewed work from the IDC and/or tech support team and made any required changes. When we were satisfied with the results, we approved the materials and returned them to the IDC who was in charge of final production.

I think that the IDC is a bit frustrated with the productions we ask him to complete. Most of the documents are written, even though we have produced a few diagrams (graphical representations). In terms of animations, we don't have many, because the professor wants more time to think about what he wants done, i.e. nice to have versus must have. Consequently, the production team moves slowly, which is unfortunate. I see again that too many resources have been allocated to production and too few to design: a waste of resources because one cannot produce what has not yet been designed.

And thus ended this course. We succeeded in building this course in six months, from top to bottom. It wasn't perfect and there was still a lot to work on, like the accessories, but for the most part, the work was done and the course could be delivered.

Ex Post Facto Interview

On the design process: "I found it very enjoyable, not only the design, but the entire process which allowed me to reflect on my course. I found the process long, but it helped me in organizing my course differently. I was constantly reflecting on why I do this and why I do that. We sometimes take things for granted. After a while, we even stop asking ourselves questions anymore."

On individual activities: "I have been teaching this course for 15 years. It is fundamentally the same, but some parts have been emphasized, others subordinated. Everything I have taught is there... an internal re-engineering of the course. (What's new?) It is more based on students' individual activities. In the past, it was more focused on my presentations. With the questions being asked, students are forced to find information rather than having the professor give it to them."

On the students: "We were already proceeding by questions, but these were not documented. And the course's clientele changed en route. This course was intended for students (in my field of study) and then I was told it had to be designed for students who only wanted an overview. I had to change everything. Other objectives, other tools!"

On individual activities: "Previously, in class, I would spontaneously raise questions. I had never written these questions down. With this approach [the design model], my students have to prepare themselves in advance. Given the model we're using, they really have to prepare themselves. But habits are hard to break and I find time is being wasted since students only prepare themselves to take notes, rather than prepare themselves to discuss the material."

On student autonomy: "It depends on the individual student. I believe that we can try out this model gradually and see what the results are, but it's up to the student to adapt. If after 5 years of university studies, they are [still] not ready to work autonomously, they might not be in the right place. Whatever method [sic] is used, there will be dead wood. If the model works for the majority of students, so be it. This model does not promote facilitating the student in his work. It requires the student's full involvement. Our students are often criticised [by my colleagues] in that they have difficulty functioning on their own, in conducting research, in finding answers. Any model that requires students to work, that forces them to reflect, is good. The student must learn to operate autonomously. Our students are already graduates. The courses are therefore graduate level. They already have at least 4 years of university."

On working in teams: "In the beginning, I wasn't very keen on their working in teams. Some work harder than others. I am still not convinced of the merits of this approach from an assessment point of view. On the other hand, I like the fact that they discuss subject matter as a group. It's good to see them discussing in groups. So long as there are no marks involved, fine. Those who are lazy or unprepared for discussions will be left aside. I believe in formative assessment for teams and in summative assessment for individuals."

On teamwork in their profession: "Yes, they must work hand-in-hand with their colleagues. Part of their work is done as a team, but in the end, they also have to bear individual responsibility for their work. In terms of planning, yes, it's done in teams. They are marked on their level of planning ability. Teamwork prepares them for learning how to plan well. Organizing/planning team assignments should be part of their training."

On the design process: "It was a new experience for me to work with an instructional designer. Enriching and interesting. The fact that you can sit with someone specialized in design... you asked me questions that no one had ever asked me before. No one had ever asked me these types of questions. Why do that? Why emphasize this aspect? ... I would do it without asking myself why... So I've improved some things and I enjoy that."

On a major problem encountered: "It was the change in clientele [sic]. That changed everything. Developing material for a certain clientele, putting time into it, then changing everything... it was like working backwards. We should have designed the course for our regular students, and then adapt the material as needed for other students. Creating a customized course takes too much time. We may have to build 4 or 5 versions of the course without a guarantee that the clientele will be there. Some courses do not change, such as a history course, but in my area of study, the course must be adapted to specific needs... such as using relevant case studies for students."

On workload: "It was hard going to design this course. We would meet for an hour and a half to three hours every week. That's practically a full course load. The horizontal course plan helped and ended up producing a better course. I often refer back to it,... but associating an objective to content and activities is demanding. It is long and sometimes frustrating to realize that we have activities for which there are no objectives. [...] Preparing this course is like giving a course. I reserved half a day every week for this work."

On problems with reading material: "The students have hundreds of pages to read, between 1,000 and 1,500 pages per term. On campus, they get their texts from the 'reserve' [in the library] and then photocopy them. With an online course, everything would have to be put online and that's the problem. Re-entering and reformatting data is a huge job but if we don't do it, there is a copyright issue linked to format. The texts themselves exist and are public domain. Also, some texts are only available from publishers but the new ones are available online. This makes it easier. But student attitudes also need to change... most of the students want hard copies."

On future course designing: "As for the course itself, I would have designed it as a regular course like I offer on campus."

On working at a distance: "Screen-sharing is definitely a plus. I really like working directly on the text like that."

On teaching online with the synchronous platform: "I really liked the direct contact with the students. [The synchronous platform] is far better than videoconferencing but I do like being able to see to whom I am speaking. I fear that online learning is becoming too mechanical. With a [web] camera on the computer, it would really enhance the visual aspect."

On accessibility to online courses and the interest in offering them: "For students in remote areas or far away, yes, I would accept to do this [teach online]. If there are no other solutions and if the bursary system isn't abolished, yes, to increase access, I would offer my courses online. [But] we have to make sure that all of the tools and documents are available online, especially since the on-campus students have access to their professors and a full library. But if there are no other means, if the quality is there, and if they have access to the necessary means for their learning, yes, online learning would be OK."

On the professor's role: "The professor provides the framework for training and must complete it with resources. The professor assists with the method, but the students must complete it by conducting their own research. No professor can say that he/she covers all the material. That is why we have libraries, computer labs, etc. If a student is led to believe that contact with the professor in class is enough, then s-he's being led astray."

On the future of faculty: "I hope that this virtual world doesn't replace the professor. Some students need the contact but I believe we can adopt a hybrid approach whereby the student comes to class and also uses distance education tools. I wouldn't want the process to become dehumanized, where the professor goes to his office and spends the day typing on his computer."

On technology and face to face teaching: "An approach is needed that responds to two types of students. In terms of my on-campus students, I wouldn't want them to stop coming to class... I wouldn't want to lose this contact that we have together. But for a student in, say, Nunavut, it would be absurd to make him come here to learn. Some aspects (in my field of study) have already integrated ICT. There is no reason to prevent the virtual from replacing the face-to-face, but I would be very disappointed as a professor to never see a student again, or have a student ever see me. In the classroom, with 40 or 50 students in front of me, I can tell if the one way in the back of the class has understood me or not. I can immediately tell this by his reaction. He may not want to ask questions for all sorts of reasons. Through eye-to-eye contact, students who may have a question but may not want to ask it are visible. Eye-to-eye contact is so important that I take the time to look at their faces, to make sure they have understood me. With online teaching, how can we manage that? I would not want face-to-face contact to disappear. It would be better to find a happy medium, between face-to-face and online learning."

CASE STUDY 10
INTEGRATING TECHNOLOGY

Case Characteristics

This professor (F) was mid-way in her career (M) and had decided to get involved in the course design process for personal reasons (P) (see Table 15). She didn't feel prepared to teach an online course before next year (3) but was relatively available to start the design work (2), which allowed for a higher number of sessions than the norm (7). She knew little about course design and had never taught an online course (1/1). Finally, her general objectives and specific objectives (GOs and SOs) were, on average, relatively more developed than those of the other professors (3).

Table 15: Characteristics of the subject matter expert

Gender	Rank	Reason	Time	Availability	No. of sessions	K/ Design	K/ DE	GO/ SO
F	ASC	P	3	2	7	1	1	3

Gender: female

Profile: ASC = associate

Reason: P = personal

Time-to-delivery: 3 = in over 4 months

Availability: 2 = 16 to 30 hours

Number of sessions = 7

Knowledge of Design: 1 = novice level

Knowledge of DE/OL: 1 = has never offered courses via DE or OL

General Obj. /Specific Obj.:
3 = GO + SO (SO in limited number)

Before our first meeting, she sent me a copy of her course syllabus and let me know she could free up one or two hours per week over the next four months to devote to course design.

I met with the new IDC assigned to this course to explain how I envisaged our collaborating on this project. Since it was the first time she's done this type of work, I provided her with a flowchart, outlining the activities to be completed, the time allotted for each, their sequence, and the *deliverables* expected from each activity. This time, I intended to keep the IDC up to speed to avoid any feelings of alienation which I felt had occurred in other cases (and for which I was feeling responsible).

One day, during an earlier course, one of the IDCs with whom I had been working told me that he suddenly had too much work to do in the time he had left, after several weeks of non-production. It is true that sometimes

my work with professors didn't always quickly produce didactic material ready to be produced by the IDC. Objectives need to be defined, activities have to be designed, in short, the foundation of the 'house' has to be poured before we can start on the framework. It's always the image of an architect that comes to mind when I think about design, the architect who produces nothing but paper for weeks (or months) on end. But is not this paper essential for construction/production to begin? It is unfortunate that the IDCs are under the impression that they must sit around and wait for me to give them work to do. Once again, it seems to me that this is a human resources problem. Normally, the IDC should be in the process of completing one project while the ID is starting up another one. It seems that management fails to understand the instructional design process as a whole, which perpetuates misunderstandings. Moreover, as the sole senior designer (with a junior in training), I'm often rushed off my feet to get something to the IDCs who seem to have all of the time in the world to get their work done. A reallocation of resources, such as in another senior designer and maybe one less IDC, would go a long way to alleviating this problem.

Session 1: I started by introducing myself and describing my role in the process and then asked the professor to tell me about her course, its position in the program, and so on.

Through experience, I have come to understand how important it is, from the very first meeting, to create a working climate that fosters several intangibles: a sense of confidentiality (this is why I carefully explain the instructional designer's ethics of professional conduct on confidentiality), a sense of belonging to the current project (as both of us are committed to a common-interest process), recognizing the professor's expertise on content while recognizing the designer's technical expertise in terms of faculty development and andragogy (the professors must trust the ID to support them), all of which emphasize the importance of having experienced IDs involved (ideally with a graduate degree in ID and university-level teaching experience). It seems to me that it is only when this type of climate has been established that the work can begin and continue in a productive manner.

She began explaining to me that her course was one of the first courses undergraduate students take in their program. It is what might be called a *leveller*, a course that develops a solid foundation for the students in subsequent courses. It was also a course that this particular professor had been giving for at least ten years. She stated that she constantly changed the didactic resources she used. We then began reviewing her current course syllabus. I talked to her about the sequence of activities she had planned for each week. Her plan was relatively well constructed in that she had already identified, in some detail, course-related activities each week. But there were no specific objectives and her content was described in rather general themes. She explained that she liked to be able to change things quickly, and that if she prepared things too far in advance, she felt she might feel cornered by planning that was too rigid and not truly respectful of the students she had in class that term who certainly had particular and specific needs.

> *It's not the first time I have heard this argument. A principle of constructivist pedagogy is indeed to give free rein (or at least some margin for manoeuvre) to students in defining their own learning activities. The principle is fine in itself and it indicates a certain level of caring on the part of professors who use this argument. But, by the same token, it could also be used as a pretext to avoid quite a bit of planning (which is admittedly tiresome). I must therefore try to think of a way of outflanking this argument if we are to get any work done...*

I answered her by asking a question: "Is the aim for all of the students to acquire a minimum number of competencies?" She answered in the affirmative, so I followed up by asking how, if all of the students were, in principle, to succeed in achieving the same level of competency, she intended to organize her course so that this would occur. She felt she could adapt her course to every group of students she met. This would mean that some students would be better prepared than others to take her course. It would also indicate that her course requirements would vary depending on the strengths of any particular group of students. The marks students would get would therefore likely reflect normative assessment rather than criterion-based assessment, something with which she said she had difficulty in her department. Consequently, I suggested she build a basic course for all of her students and then add supplementary activities for those individuals who were stronger than the average, capable of going further into the subject matter, as well as compensatory exercises for the weaker students. This all boiled down to doing more design earlier on, instead of less. We finally agreed on creating a basic course and having a bank of resources which students could access depending on their specific needs. We ended our meeting with my presenting the HCP model.

She did seem a bit upset with our discussion even though she said she was happy with the result of our session. I think that the emphasis on the pedagogical approach caught her off guard. Even though she was obviously a very experienced professor and deeply committed to her students, I got the impression that our exchanges left her feeling somewhat out of her league. I already found this in working with other faculty members. Instructional design seems to disrupt a lot of their thinking about teaching because the process generates a lot of questions and creates uncertainty in areas where certitude had reigned. I realize that this is difficult for some so I try to limit what I say to the bare essentials during our first session. However, certain realities are inescapable. During the first session, I often find myself guessing who will continue and who will drop out of the process. As for this professor, I have no doubts. Even though she is shaken (even stirred), she does want to pursue it further.

Session 2: Our session began where we left off: reviewing her current course syllabus and transferring elements to the HCP. She recognized that she had not developed all of her general objectives, so we spent a good part of our time defining and allocating them—a relatively easy step in the process since she had already defined many. What was missing was their weekly distribution throughout the syllabus.

That is one of the things that frustrate me the most in this type of work: current course syllabus models do not require that professors situate or contextualize their objectives. Consequently, most professors simply content themselves with drafting a few, often a mix of GOs and SOs, and adding them at the beginning of their syllabus. I often see a whole list of specific objectives without any reference to any particular activity... Just a list of objectives, one after the other, reminding me of the folksong, "Little Boxes."

We then took a look at the course's fifteen weeks, taking out the first week during which she presents her course syllabus, then removing Spring or Fall Break (called "Reading Week" in French Canada...how much reading actually gets done?), and then the final week, for a course synthesis or a final exam. Thus, we end with twelve weeks of actual learning time, for which objectives must be set and instructional activities planned. So we started to develop general objectives and distribute them vertically over this twelve-week period, from the second week (save break week) to the fourteenth. Next, we moved along to the specific objectives of Week 2. And, as usual, I questioned the professor about the activities she expected her students to complete outside of class between Weeks 1 and 2. She was not planning to have them work in teams at the beginning, preferring to wait until Week 3 or 4 while the class stabilizes (as "course shoppers" come and go). I felt that was a wise decision and made a note-to-self. Despite the musical chairs, she expected her students to do the required readings before coming to class. Based on her explanations, I proposed the following objectives:

- From the required reading, define the subject area's key concepts.
- Identify the logical sequence of concepts.
- Explain the reasoning behind concept linkages.

She said she was satisfied with her objectives in that she felt they reflected the individual assignment that the students would have to complete in preparation for the Week 2 plenary. We continued in the same manner for Week 3: determining the week's specific objectives, elaborating on the resources needed to achieve them, and writing out individual activities (supported by existing resources). We repeated the process for Weeks 4 and 5 and then started writing up team activities—a laborious task because this professor had never before developed this type of activity.

Just like most of the professors involved in this development research project, summative evaluation had always been the norm for her as well as individual student performance evaluation. She did have her students work together in class as teams but it was so that they could prepare to complete the course requirements individually. I explained the constructivist philosophy rationale, adding that, according to this approach, working in teams is considered to be much more than a means to an end. It is, for the learners, a way to build and develop knowledge. I usually stop talking about constructivism when I begin to see a professor's eyes rolling, as if to say, that's all well and good, but I have other fish to fry... (i.e. better things to do than develop team activities).

Session 3: We continued planning, working from her own syllabus and going back and forth between it and the HCP. She said she really liked the model's precision, but found that we spent a lot of time planning, too much time which, in her opinion, could have been better spent actually producing tools such as multimedia presentations. I explained that identifying her objectives was the most useful thing to do because these objectives would guide the development of everything else. We couldn't have an effect without a cause. Hence, writing up objectives was an essential step, for we would never know *what* to produce if we didn't first know what it was intended to achieve.

I now have a vague impression that I'm like the one who pours the concrete for the foundation of the house. The owner, who drives by his house, only sees a pile of dirt and a big hole. The foundation, while essential, doesn't have as much glamour as the finished house—the pretty little windows and the hardwood floors—and, to make matters worse, concrete takes its good old time drying.

Getting back to the role of the ID and to the metaphor of the architect, the latter must often get the feeling that, in spite of his erudition, everything he produces is no more than ideas on paper, anything but concrete. The professor, however, continues to follow the design model that I am proposing, in the spirit of a leap of faith, but I can see that her patience is wearing thin and that she'd rather we move on to something more "concrete"!

It was at this point that I saw that a substantial part of her course could be done by her students working on their own and that a large number of the objectives could be reached using over-the-counter software. I now started thinking about how I could break it to her gently. I explained that, in almost every subject area, there was now specialized software to assist students in attaining the more elementary objectives in courses autonomously. Generally unfamiliar with computers, even less so with software, she was not aware of any software that would apply to her course. So we did some online research, looking at similar course syllabi in other universities and at the resources available to students. We also searched for learning support programs. In no time at all, we found inexpensive software (roughly $50) that would enable students to practice certain skills as often as they liked. She placed an order directly online for a sample demonstration. Now that's concrete!

But with discovery came disillusionment. She feared that an important part of her course, even her entire course, risked being cancelled with the introduction of software. On a positive note, I impressed upon her that even their using instructional software would still only allow them to meet some of the objectives—namely the lower order objectives—of her course. So this simply meant re-engineering her course to factor in an important resource, one that her students would likely continue to use after their studies were completed. More and more it appeared, employers expected graduates, the workers of the future, to be computer science savvy in whatever field they worked. This launched a long discussion about the relevance of introducing students to tools that are universal and applicable to almost any context versus the relevance of simply teaching discipline-related principles with limited application. What indeed is the mandate of universities? We concluded that universities should aim at doing two things: generally developing critical thinking and judgment among students as well as properly equipping them with marketable skills so they might enter the job market with confidence.

Session 4: We moved forward with the software trial, assessed our findings on its usefulness and began integrating it into her course syllabus. That was it! There was nothing more to say. We made a few adjustments, especially during the first weeks of the course, making sure students had the instructions they would need to use the software. Using most of her current activities from her existing syllabus, we tweaked her individual exercises, adapted some of them to the software and succeeded, one by one, in completing the first five weeks of her course. We finished by setting out all of our GOs and SOs. We were on a roll!

Sessions 5-6-7: Work on the assignments continued, the routine was set. We moved along methodically, week by week. We added resources from her documentary bank (mostly texts), and finished adjusting the Individual Assignments as well as completing a Team Assignment for every two weeks of class. She still had doubts about developing these team activities but a lot fewer than when we began meeting.

Session 8: The HCS was now complete, the objectives designed, the didactic materials gathered, the individual and team activities finished. We started planning the weekly plenary sessions and carefully prepared the steps for the very first plenary (the most important one). The professor decided to focus on student motivation in taking the course, showing the relevance, utility and importance of this field of study. She is thinking of using an educational game she found online to break the ice, so to speak. Apparently, the shift to the cyber world has taken hold.

Sessions 9-10: We carried on with planning the plenary sessions and associated activities. We adopted the hourglass approach as introduced in Case 7; that is, every week, she would review the week's assignments (both individual and team), targeting the main problems encountered, answering individual and team questions as they came up and then introducing next week's themes and activities.

This was where my development research project ended, with this case study. I believed I had finally found a model that effectively guided subject matter experts (professors) to using instructional design principles to create online courses within a reasonable timeframe and while expending a reasonable amount of effort. The result was promising. Hopefully, future studies will critique, elaborate upon and develop some of the practices developed in this book.

Ex Post Facto Interview

On motivation to explore DE: "When I started thinking about distance education, I said to myself: "I am ready to explore things a bit without giving it my 100 percent. So we started the sessions and I enjoyed them.

I realized that it was possible to do the things I had always wanted to do, but for which I had never made time."

On analyzing her course syllabus:"I really liked the way we started the process. We looked at my course syllabus together and you showed me the HCS model. I could see where I could improve on my current syllabus—it was all very relaxed; there was no criticism of what was already there. I found that really positive."

On writing objectives: "Obviously, writing instructional objectives has always been my pet peeve. They are difficult to write. It seems as though we never get to write out everything we actually do in class. Sometimes I get the impression that the objectives are too minute, too small if you will, even insignificant, and are not representative of everything my students achieve or produce in a class. But I believe it is a worthwhile exercise, even if is hard to do. It makes us focus on the essentials and leave behind the rest. It's a good exercise that requires discipline."

On the horizontal course syllabus: "I like dividing the course into separate parts, one week at a time. In my usual course syllabus, there are certain divisions and I have a pretty good idea of what I am going to do every week, but the horizontal plan allowed me to be clearer and more precise. So I think this was a big advantage for my students. And by relying on my syllabus, I know where I am in my subject matter. The only thing that bothered me was how crazy it was getting it designed. Heck, it's OK now... I'm just glad now that it's over and done."

On how the course is organized: "As for course content, I had in the past kept things rather loose, in case I came upon something I wanted to add to the course at the last minute. Often, right in the middle of a term, I would find an article, a chapter or a copy of something that I wanted to share with my students. As you know, we're always searching for something new to show our students but, now that my course is designed, I can see the usefulness of planning, but also of enriching and improving it along the way. [Having the course designed], that is something one can at least be sure of. And I also realized I would have to limit the number of readings and assignments I was asking of my students. Having my course spread out before me on a grid made me understand that not everything was essential. So the exercise of seeing the entire course in a grid allowed me to remove some of the documents and activities. Seeing that I didn't have any objectives linked to this or that reading made me ask myself, "Now, why would I ask them to do that?"

On working in teams vs. working individually: "Individual assignments have always been the focal point of my course. I never had any really good experiences having students work in teams. It's as though there were always complaints to deal with about the students who did not work well with others. It was heavy and tiring. I admit that it is just less complicated having them work individually but, after talking it over and considering the constructivist learning approach, etc., I started reconsidering my position. It just might be worthwhile."

On individual assignments and team assignments: "Together, we reviewed my material and we saw that a lot of the exercises that the students worked on individually could be done in teams. I also liked the idea of drafting questions based on the readings, something I never had time to do before. And having them compare their answers to the Individual Assignments within their teams before coming to class, I think was a good idea since it made them focus more on the subject matter. That worked and the students seem to understand the readings better. This year, in any case, I noticed a difference. We discussed themes more in class and the students seemed more prepared. The results for this term aren't in yet, but I wouldn't be surprised if they were better."

On having her documents on the Web: "I know that students like working like that. Many have told me that if they forget something, they can always get to my site and find it. It's also fun because I always forget to tell them something in class. I get home and then I remember what it was. So now, all I have to do is add it to the bulletin board on my website. I really like that!"

On changing her pedagogy: "My classes have also changed. I have more time in class to discuss things with my students. At first, I wondered what I would do in class now that they have all the resources they need, documents to read, exercises and the rest. I was a little concerned...I was thinking about it a lot. I was in the habit of talking, talking, talking during my classes. I'm like that. There is so much material to cover in any case, but it's worked out well. We now have time to go into details. For some students, it's always the same thing. They come to class and expect me to talk for 3 hours. They probably made me the lecturer I am. I am aware of that. I think you need to know how to use silence as a pedagogical tool. It can sometimes get uncomfortable, but it takes time and patience to change routines, theirs as well as ours. So, I think that with all the resources that I've put on my website, I will become less of a lecturer in my teaching. At least, I hope so."

On the lack of time: "My course now is just about where I want it to be, but it took two terms to get it there. And it's only one of my courses. It's true that some of the texts that I posted on the asynchronous platform can also be used in other courses. That's still to be seen. I would like to know more about using the asynchronous platform. For the moment, the team uploads my files to it but I feel handicapped. I want to be autonomous, but I find it complicated. I am not a computer whiz so it takes me a while to master new applications. Time is what's missing. If I had more time, I would do it."

On the future: "I am quite sure that I will continue to develop material to post on the asynchronous platform. It's so practical—I don't have to get documents photocopied and distributed. The students like it too. They all have computers or come to the lab whenever they want."

On teaching face-to-face: "In terms of leaving my face-to-face classes, I don't feel quite ready yet. I want to explore doing parts of my course online using the synchronous platform. I find it easy enough to use and I think that my students will like using it. The trials that I did were quite interesting but I don't see myself using it as long as my students can get to campus. If we want to attract out-of-town enrolments, it would certainly be a means. For now though, we haven't discussed it in my department."..."But I would find it difficult not to see my students. I like seeing them and discussing with them. It's hard to replace face-to-face teaching. If we don't have a choice, we can get organized, but it remains to be seen how it will work out in the long term."

Synthesis and final prototype

I started this study with one goal in mind: developing an instructional design prototype model adapted to the needs of faculty working at a dual-mode university. It began with the normal stages of instructional design as found in the literature and combined current course planning practices among faculty. Out of this combination, an initial prototype model was elaborated an implemented in Case 1. This first case was fairly typical of distance education courses that are developed in organisations where there is low-level infrastructure for doing so and where such courses often have to be designed and developed in a hurry for almost immediate delivery. In Case 1, the professor was a new professor, he had little knowledge of either design or of distance education and he was required to develop his course for distance delivery because of an existing department obligation *vis-à-vis* off-campus students.

As the study moved forward to Cases 2 and 3, a pattern began to emerge with regard to how the design work was being accomplished: there was only a short delay between course design and course delivery and the professors did not seem entirely committed to the process. At times, they seemed even hostile to it, undoubtedly because of the organisational constraints under which they were working. The result of these constraints (such as administration-set deadlines for course delivery) was the emergence of a rapid instructional design model prototype. Making matters significantly more difficult was the fact that for most of these professors, this was the first time they had ever worked with an ID and a technical support team to develop their course for distance delivery. Having little or no idea of what to expect and being required to prepare for something they had never done, several faculty members experienced high levels of stress. They therefore saw the entire process as one which was in addition to their normal tasks. These factors combined to create what might accurately be termed as an "agitated design conditions."

It was during these first cases that the limits of the initial prototype became obvious and that it underwent several rapid evolutions after being tested and retested in rapid sequence in conditions that required prompt action and subsequent prototype adjustment. This interactive, design research approach resulted rather quickly in a viable prototype emerging by case 3 and being implemented in case 4, a prototype which increasingly reflected professor needs and limits. The prototype would continue to undergo changes between Case 4 to 10 but they were only minor in nature. Indeed, Case 3 was pivotal in that the lessons learned during it set the stage for major changes to the prototype and applied during Case 4. It was thus during Cases 3 and 4 that the prototype began reflecting various levels of design depending on the institutional constraints imposed upon it, namely the amount of time available for design and the amount of effort professors were able to expend.

Case 5 was another example of the ID and professor working furiously to redesign a course which resulted in their applying only part of the prototype out a lack of time. Case 6 was unique unto itself in that the professor did not fit the usual professor profile as seen thus far. His personal characteristics such as his background and experience were such that they set him apart from his colleagues. For these reasons, this case was seen as being atypical yet, nevertheless, it did allow the ID to test various aspects of the prototype which may not have been tested had not this particular professor profile emerged at this particular time. Indeed, the difference in profile allowed the ID to establish what was absolutely essential in the prototype and what could be removed.

Case 7 was timely in that, given the professor's characteristics and the ardour with which he applied himself to his work, it brought new elements to the prototype as well as allowing the ID to work in an unfettered fashion, being unhindered by time or other limits, and fully apply the prototype and verify the principles by which it worked. Case 8 once again propelled the prototype forward under ideal conditions, namely time to work systematically and Case 9 reminded the ID of the importance of not only making sure that the course was adequately designed and developed but that it was also properly delivered. Case 10 showed signs of data saturation in that no further changes were made to the prototype. Finally, Figure 8 presents the evolving design of the prototype, from its creation before Case 1 to its earliest changes in Cases 3 and 4, from its emerging final form in Case 4 and 5 to the last changes made to it in Case 9.

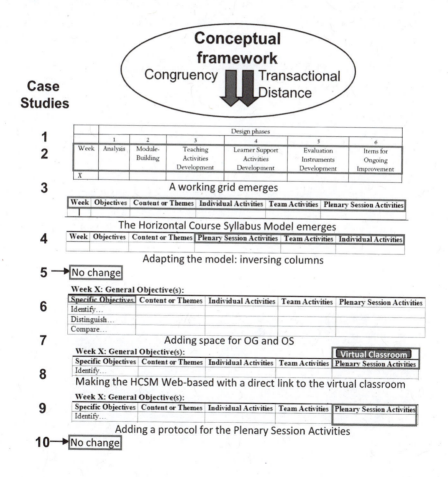

Figure 8: The design model prototype and its transformation throughout the ten case studies

Figure 9 presents the most recent version of the prototype which is the final result of this study. Just as the varied and specific needs of faculty emerged and the prototype evolved and was articulated in response to such, it is expected that the design models instructional designers use will also vary in nature and degree. The contrary would be disastrous for the development of online learning for it is the IDs whose job it is to identify design-related problems and, by reflecting on their practice, to develop relevant and effective educational solutions. As IDs play this vital role, we can expect a real flowering of online learning and of the online learner.

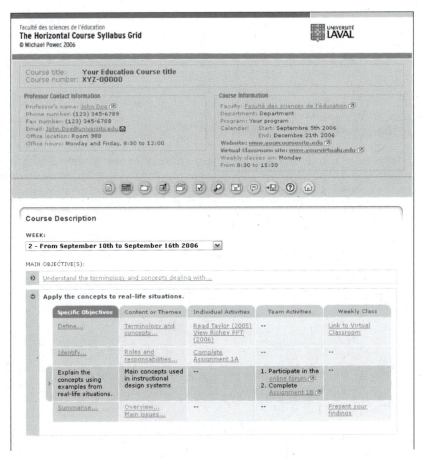

Figure 9: The current version of the design prototype (Power, 2008a)

Conclusion

This is the end of a process, momentary in nature, akin to a round in the ring. No knock-out punch has been delivered, not even a technical KO but some degree of success has been achieved. After a particularly rough round, the boxers stagger off to their corners, attend to their wounds and wait for the bell announcing the next round.

Just like a story without an ending, the online course design process is endless. We must continue on, we must make progress, we must innovate and we must talk about it! What is especially needed is our documenting what we do as IDs and how we do it. This is the kind of research that allows any field to move forward, to avoid dead-ends and to pave new promising avenues. Research is no longer the yoke of the accredited researcher but the work of many contributing workers, those who do the work and who know the trials involved; those who live them first-hand. Everything may be of value; the smallest bit of information may turn out to be what unravels the secret to successful online teaching and learning. Throughout this exploration of the online universe, our sole compass is our solidarity. Collaboration takes on an added urgency in this vast space which is virtually unlimited.

Hoping to hear from you...

Michael

Epilogue

As the original, French-language, edition of this book went to press, the design model continued to evolve. So, in order to give readers an update on developments, I have decided to add this epilogue to the English-language version of the book.

Indeed, I am indebted to MERLOT and the editors of the *Journal of Online Teaching and Learning*, Number 4, Volume 4) for allowing me to use the *Discussion* and *Conclusion* sections of my Dec. 15, 2008 article below. This section will bring the reader up to speed with regard to the latest developments of the design prototype which I am now calling the *Blended Online Learning Environment*.

This study demonstrated that, for a successful design prototype to be successfully implemented in a traditional university setting, it had to be based on low "structure" and high "dialog" (Moore, 1993) and must emulate traditional university practices and operations. This is supported by Jaffee's (1998) conclusion that:

> The receptivity and perceived legitimacy of new educational delivery modes is strongly related to the extent to which these instructional technologies reinforce or retain the central

elements of the institutionalized and identity-enhancing classroom setting. (Jaffee, 1998: p. 28).

This suggests the need for university administrators to adopt an online learning (OL) deployment model which is closely linked to traditional university course delivery operations rather than a classical, distance education (DE) design and development-focused model, essentially foreign in its functioning to traditional universities (Keegan, 1996; Rumble & Harry, 1982). Faculty would thus not only have access to a feasible means of teaching online in a manner to which they are accustomed but, more importantly, they would utilize a socioconstructivist-enabled learning environment which would be in stark contrast to the sorely criticized, behaviorist-associated, lock-step ID model as implemented worldwide by open and DE universities (Evans, 2001: Masie, 2000). Henceforth, by accessing a delivery-focused model offering both synchronous and asynchronous opportunities for exchange, students and faculty would benefit from asynchronously-accessible, Web-based tools and resources in addition to synchronously interacting in a fashion quite similar to the on-campus experience, accessing powerful audio-, video- and screen-sharing and Web browsing functions to do so (Hamilton & Cherniavsky, 2006). Moreover, faculty would experience a resumption of quality control over DE/OL which has either been delegated to surrogate actors in higher education or even quietly extirpated from the hands of faculty by increasingly prevalent and highly influential corporate interests (Magnussen, 2005; Noble, 2002).

The realization that this study brought to the author, that DE under the guise of online learning was fast approaching mainstream higher education, also brought with it, paradoxically, an insight into the decline of DE as it had been known. In its stead, OL appears to be fully emerging as a viable successor. However, the ID prototype emerging from this study was different from OL as it had been known for most of its short lifespan, i.e. the online continuation of a DE-based, pre-designed, anywhere-anytime, asynchronous, individual student-paced learning environment (Harasim, 1995; Hiltz, Teles & Turoff, 1995; Hiltz & Goldman, 2005). The emerging prototype was a blend of the past and the future, on the one hand hearkening back to an era when teaching and learning always occurred simultaneously in time and in space (in the classroom) but, on the other hand, reaching forward under its new guise to an era of borderless, networked, online communications freed from the limits of space, indicative of a reported shift from structural to relational considerations in OL (Garrison, 2000). In experiencing new freedom from old limits, it was observed that faculty became cognizant of their reassertion of direct ownership of their teaching and student support duties which, in the classical DE model, had been typically delegated to tutors (Mason, 1979).

Throughout this study, the design and technical team had to balance concerns expressed firstly by administration and their concern for increasing levels of cost-effective outreach and, secondly, by faculty, primarily concerned with instructional quality, technical support and overall workload management issues. As the asynchronous and synchronous components of this environment were fully integrated and an understanding of the implications of doing so matured, the author realized that the simultaneous blending of a synchronous environment with an asynchronous course management system produced a variation of the campus-based, *blended learning* model, as defined by Garrison & Vaughan (2008):

> The basic principle [of blended learning] is that face-to-face oral communication and online written communication are optimally integrated such that the strengths of each are blended into a unique learning experience congruent with the context and intended educational purpose (Garrison & Vaughan, 2008: p. 42).

The completely online solution – termed *online e-learning* by Piskurich – was subsequently termed the *blended online learning environment*, it being the natural extension of both *blended learning* as defined by Garrison & Vaughan (2008) and *online learning* as defined, for instance, by http://www. aln.org/. In Figure 10, the *blended online learning environment* design model is described as the completely online, simultaneous and complimentary integration and implementation of an asynchronous-mode, partially system-managed, partially faculty-led learning environment (i.e. a course management system, or CMS) and a synchronous-mode, partially system-managed, partially faculty-led learning environment (i.e. a virtual classroom environment).

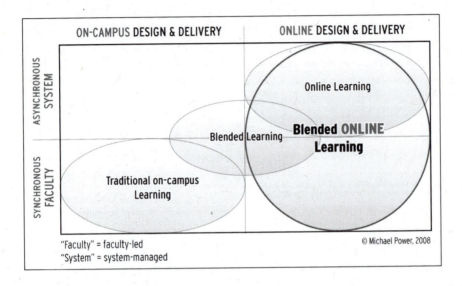

Figure 10: The relative position of Blended Online Learning

In more detail, the traditional, faculty-led, campus-based course teaching/learning model (in the bottom left-hand corner) is juxtaposed, on the x-axis, with the asynchronous online teaching/learning model (in the top right-hand corner). Along the y-axis, faculty-led instruction, usually synchronous and taking place on campus (bottom left-hand side of the figure), is juxtaposed with asynchronous system-led instruction, i.e. online, tutor-supported instruction, common in open and distance university course delivery models (top right-hand side of the figure). The circles "traditional on-campus learning" (including teaching) and "online learning" represent, respectively, the width and breadth of each system within its own sphere. *Blended learning* is seen here as bridging both spheres, increasingly existing in numerous and varied forms (Bonk & Graham, 2006; Garrison & Vaughan, 2008; Mortera-Gutierrez, 2006). Finally, *blended online learning* is seen as bridging both asynchronous and synchronous forms of instruction, thereby occupying the whole of the OL space.

This environment represents a series of trade-offs between high-level and high quality but equally highly-priced, front end-designed Web courses and high-level dialogue, albeit cost-prohibitive, videoconferencing-delivered courses. As such, it combines faculty attainable- and sustainable-level structure via the asynchronous learning environment and sustainable-level, faculty-student dialog via the synchronous learning environment. It also represents a low learning curve approach to faculty online migration and an administration-friendly, cost-effective approach to increasing university outreach.

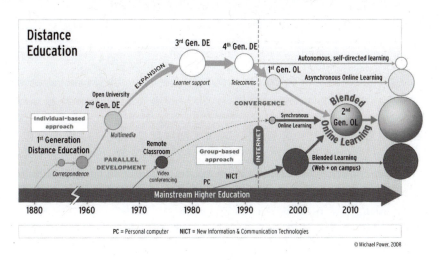

Figure 11. The emergence of Blended Online Learning

As a result of these developments, the author began reflecting on changes occurring in the entire field of distance education. In Figure 11, the emergence of the blended online learning environment is set in the overall context of DE and OL. It is posited here that DE as a field is currently undergoing a major shift in impetus and expansion. For well over a century, DE, a subset of mainstream higher education (Moore & Kearsley, 2004), is now emerging as a major force worldwide, but under a new guise. OL is seen as the successor of DE, the natural outgrowth of the field, fuelled by the Internet and by increasingly pervasive, available and cost-effective information and communication technologies (McGreal & Elliott, 2008). It is furthermore posited that first-generation

OL, after a decade of trial and error during which time it was known mainly as an asynchronous-based form of education (Hiltz & Goldman, 2005; Twigg, 2004), is currently entering its second generation, that of *blended online learning*, a generation characterized by the *redesign* of university courses (Garrison & Vaughan, 2008). As a result, increasingly numerous forms of blended learning are currently being implemented on campuses throughout North America (Park & Bonk, 2006), combining various kinds of OL activities and culminating in what is termed the *blended online learning environment*. It should be noted that the so-called fifth generation of DE (Taylor, 2001) has intentionally not been included here as it is felt that it might better be described as *first-generation online learning*.

To sum up, the results of this study suggest that, in short, 1) faculty are increasingly encouraged to support university outreach by their administration (Dudestadt, Atkins & Van Howseling, 1999); 2) as they do so, they are encountering obstacles which prevent their applying the classical DE model (Sammons & Ruth, 2007) and 3) new technological means are reacquainting faculty with "continuity of practice" in their pedagogy (Power, 2008b). Because synchronous-mode, virtual classrooms are not yet mainstream in higher education (Keegan, Schwenke, Fritsch, Kenny, Kismihok, Biro, Gabor, O'Suilleabhain, & Nix, 2005; Ng, 2007), more research, especially field research (Abrami & Bernard, 2006), into this promising field of inquiry is important. This study, based directly on field observations and documented case studies, introduces the blending online learning environment concept and identifies its import to higher education, alluding also to possible positive effects on the field of instructional design and technology. It is felt that this study contributes to sparse yet necessary research for sustainable and cost-effective university outreach as well as to effective human and material resources deployment.

More specifically, this study addresses a need for a teaching and learning environment that accurately reflects faculty realities, providing both a resource-rich structure and multiple opportunities for both real-time and differed dialog between learners as well as between learners and faculty. It suggests that there is a need for balance between the aims of administration, faculty limits and learner needs and it establishes bottom-line requirements for structure and dialogue in a workable teaching-learning environment. It is posited that this can be achieved by blending newly-available information and communication technologies (ICT) to provide online learners with a complete OL environment, faculty with a feasible alternative to restrictive on-campus teaching and administration with the means to manage responsible outreach. Despite some research design-related limits (limited sample, on-going studies), the findings and related theorizations in this article may enable designers, faculty members as well as administrators to better understand and act upon some of the basic issues surrounding the design, redesign and delivery of blended online learning.

Bibliography

Abrami, P.C., Bernard, R.M., Wade, C.A., Schmid, R.F., Borokhovski,E., Tamim, R., Surkes, M., Lowerison, G., Zhang, D., Nicolaidou, I., Newman, S., Wozney, L. & Peretiatkowicz, A. (2006). *A Review of E-learning in Canada: A Rough Sketch of the Evidence, Gaps and Promising Directions*. Montreal: Centre for the Study of Learning and Performance, April 3.

Anderson, T., Ed. (2008). *Theory and Practice of Online Learning*. Athasbasca, AB: Athabasca University. http://www.aupress.ca/books/ Terry_Anderson.php

Ausubel, D. (1963). *The Psychology of Meaningful Verbal Learning*. New York: Grune & Stratton.

Block, J. (1982). Assimilation, Accommodation, and the Dynamics of Personality Development. *Child Development*, Vol. 53, No. 2 (April), 281–295.

Bloom, B.S. (1984). *Taxonomy of educational objectives*. Boston, MA: Allyn and Bacon.

Boettcher, J. V. & Conrad, R. (2004). *Faculty guide for moving teaching and learning to the Web* (2nd ed.). Phoenix: League for Innovation in the Community College.

Bonk, C.J. & Graham, C. R., Eds. (2006). *Handbook of blended learning: Global Perspectives, local designs*. San Francisco: Pfeiffer.

Brien, R. (1992). *Design pédagogique : Introduction à l'approche de Gagné et de Briggs*. Ste-Foy, QC : Les Éditions St-Yves.

Carr-Chellman, A.A. (2005). *E-learning: rhetoric versus reality*. Thousand Oaks, CA: Sage.

Clifford, V.A. (2004). Book Review. Learning through storytelling in higher education. Using reflection and experience to improve learning. J. McDrury & M. Alterio, (2003) London: Kogan and Page. In *International Journal for Academic Development*, Vol. 10, No. 1, May, 63–70.

Colbeck, C.L. , Campbell, S. C. , & Bjorklund, S. A. (2000). Grouping in the dark: What college students learn from group projects. *Journal of Higher Education*, 71, 60–83.

Dick, W. & Carey, L. (2000). *The systematic design of instruction* (5th ed.) New York: Addison-Wesley.

Dick, W., Carey, L. & Carey, J. O. (2007). *The systematic design of instruction* (7th ed.) Boston: Allyn & Bacon/Merrill.

Duderstadt, J.J., Atkins, D.E. & Van Houweling, D. (2002). *Higher Education in the Digital Age: Technology Issues and Strategies for American Colleges and Universities*. Westport, Connecticut: Greenwood Publishing.

Duval, E., Hodgkins, W., Rehak, D. & Robson, R. (2003). Learning Objects 2003 Symposium: lessons learned, questions asked. Retrieved on Sept 14 2008: Available at: http://www.cs.kuleuven. ac.be/~erikd/PRES/2003/LO2003/index.html

Evans, T. (2001). Changing universities, changing work: A consideration of diversity, change and the (re)organisation of work in higher education. *Proceedings of the Teaching and learning conference, 2001: Tertiary teaching and learning: Dealing with diversity*, 184–196.

Fahy, P.J. (2003). Indicators of Support in Online Interaction. *The International Review of Research in Open and Distance Learning*, Vol 4, No. 1.

Flanagan, J.C. 1954. The critical incident technique. *Psychological bulletin*, 51 (4), 327–358.

Flavell, J.H. (1979). Metacognition and cognitive monitoring: A new area of cognitive-developmental inquiry. *American Psychologist*, v34, n10, 906–11, Oct.

Gagne, R. (1985). The Conditions of Learning (4th ed.). New York: Holt, Rinehart & Winston.

Gagne, R., Briggs, L. & Wager, W. (1992). *Principles of instructional design* (4th ed.). Fort Worth, TX: Harcourt Brace.

Garrison, R. (2000). Theoretical Challenges for Distance Education in the 21st Century: A Shift from Structural to Transactional Issues. *International Review of Research in Open and Distance Learning*, June. Retrieved on July 7th, 2008: http://www.irrodl.org/content/v1.1/randy.html

Garrison, D.R. & Vaughan, N. D. (2008). *Blended Learning in Higher Education: Framework, Principles, and Guidelines*. San Francisco: Jossey-Bass.

Gentner, D., & Stevens, A.L. (Eds.). (1983). *Mental models*. Hillsdale, NJ: Lawrence Erlbaum.

Gustafson, K.L. & Branch, R.M. (1997). *Survey of Instructional Development. Models*. (3rd ed.). Syracuse, NY: Information Resources Publications.

Hamilton, E.R., & Cherniavsky, J. (2006). Issues in synchronous versus asynchronous e-learning platforms. In H.F. O'Neil, & S.R. Perez (Eds.), *Web-based learning: Theory, research, and practice* (87–106). Mahwah, NJ: Erlbaum.

Harasim, L., Hiltz, R., Teles, L., & Turoff, M. (1995). *Learning Networks: A field guide to teaching and learning online*. Cambridge, MA: MIT Press.

Heath, S.B., Lapp, D, Flood, J. (2005). *Handbook of Research on Teaching Literacy through the Communicative and Visual Arts*. Mahwah, NJ: Lawrence Erlbaum.

Hiltz, S. R. & Goldman, R., Eds. (2005). *Learning Together Online: Research on Asynchronous Learning Networks*. Mahwah, NJ: Lawrence Erlbaum.

Hodgins, W. (2000). *Into the Future: A Vision Paper*. Commission on Technology & Adult Learning of the American Society for Training & Development (ASTD) and National Governors' Association (NGA).

Retrieved on September 7, 2008: http://www.learnativity.com/into_the_future2000.html

Holmberg, B. (1983). Guided didactic conversation in distance education. In D. Sewart, D. Jaffee, D. (1998). Institutionalized Resistance to Asynchronous Learning Networks. *Journal of Asynchronous Learning Networks*, Volume 2, Issue 2, September, 21–32.

Janovy, J. Jr. (2003). *Teaching in Eden: Lessons from Cedar Point*. London: Routledge Falmer.

Jonassen, D.H., Peck, K., & Wilson, B.G. (1999). *Learning with Technology: A Constructivist Perspective*. Columbus, OH: Merrill/Prentice-Hall.

Keegan, D., Schwenke, E., Fritsch, H., Kenny, G., Kismihok, G., Biro, M., Gabor, A., O'Suilleabhain, G., & Nix, J. (2005). *Virtual classrooms in educational provision: Synchronous elearning systems for European institutions*. ZIFF PAPIERE 126. Hagen, Germany: Zentrales Institut für Fernstudienforschung (ZIFF), FernUniversität, July. Retrieved April 12, 2007: http://www.fernuni-hagen.de/ZIFF/synchronous.pdf

Landa, L. (1974). *Algorithmization in Learning and Instruction*. Englewood Cliffs, NJ: Educational Technology Publications.

Laurillard, D.M. (1993). *Rethinking University Teaching: A Framework for the Effective Use of Educational Technology*. London: Routledge.

Keegan, D. (1996). *Foundations of distance education (3rd ed.)*. London & New York: Routledge.

Keegan, D., Schwenke, E., Fritsch, H., Kenny, G., Kismihok, G., Biro, M., Gabor, A., O'Suilleabhain, G., & Nix, J. (2005). *Virtual classrooms in educational provision: Synchronous elearning systems for European institutions*. ZIFF PAPIERE 126. Hagen, Germany: Zentrales Institut für Fernstudienforschung (ZIFF), FernUniversität, July. Retrieved April 12th, 2007: http://www.fernuni-hagen.de/ZIFF/synchronous.pdf

Landa, L. (1974). *Algorithmization in Learning and Instruction*. Englewood Cliffs, NJ: Educational Technology Publications.

Lee, J. & Allen, K. (2001). Good Online practices = Good online students. In *Technology is the Catalyst: Proceedings of 12th International Conference*, SITE, Orlando, 2001. Orlando: AACE.

Maeroff, G. I. (2003). *A Classroom of One: How Online Learning is Changing Our Schools and Colleges*. New York: Palgrave Macmillan.

Magnusson, J.-L. (2005). Information and Communications Technology: Plugging Ontario Higher Education into the Knowledge Society. *Encounters on Education*. Vol. 6, Fall, 119–135.

Mager, R. (1997). *Preparing Instructional Objectives*. Atlanta, Georgia: Center for Effective Performance.

Mason, J. (1979). Cooperation in course teams at the Open University. In R. Cox (Ed.), *Cooperation and choice in higher education* (pp. 53–63). London: University of London Teaching Methods Unit.

Masie, E. (2001). No More Digital Page-Turning. *E-Learning Magazine*, November 1.

Mayer, R.E.; Massa, L. (2003). Three Facets of Visual and Verbal Learners: Cognitive Ability, Cognitive Style, and Learning Preference. *Journal of Educational Psychology*, Volume 95(4), December 2003, 833–846.

McGreal, R. & Elliott, M. (2008). Technologies of Online Learning (E-learning) in T. Anderson. *The Theory and Practice of Online Learning*. Athabasca, AB: Athabasca University Press.

Merrill, MD (2002). First principles of instruction. *Educational Technology Research and Development*, 50(3), 43–59.

Millis, B.J. & Cottell, P. G. (1998). *Cooperative Learning for Higher Education Faculty*. Phoenix: Oryx Press.

Moore, M.G., & Kearsley, G. (2004). *Distance education: A systems view*, 2nd Edition. Belmont, CA: Wadsworth.

Moore, M.G. (1993). Theory of transactional distance. In D. Keegan (Ed.) *Theoretical Principles of Distance Education*. New York: Routledge.

Morissette, D. (1984). *La mesure et l'évaluation en enseignement*. Sainte-Foy, QC : Presses de l'Université Laval.

Mortera-Gutiérrez, F. (2006). Faculty Best Practices Using Blended Learning in E-Learning and Face-to-Face Instruction. *International Journal on E-Learning*. 5 (3), 313–337. Chesapeake, VA: AACE.

Mortera-Gutierrez, F. (2002). Instructor interactions in distance education environments. *Journal of Interactive Learning Research*, *13*(3), 191–209.

Ng, K. C. (2007). Replacing Face-to-Face Tutorials by Synchronous Online Technologies: Challenges and pedagogical implications. *International Review of Research in Open and Distance Learning*, Vol. 8, Number 1. March, 1–15.

Nipper, S. (1989). Third generation distance learning and computer conferencing. In R. Mason & A. Kaye (Eds.), *Mindweave: Communication, Computers and Distance Education*. Oxford: Pergamon.

Noble, D. (2002). Digital Diploma Mills: The Automation of Higher education. *First Monday*. Issue 3, Number 1. Retrieved on Sept 4th, 2006: http://www.firstmonday.org/issues/issue3_1/noble

Office québécois de la langue française (http://www.granddictionnaire.com)

Park, Y.N. & Bonk, C. J. (2007). Synchronous Learning Experiences: Distance and Residential Learners' Perspectives in a Blended Graduate Course. *Journal of Interactive Online Learning*. Volume 6, Number 3, Winter.

Park, O.C. and Hopkins, R. (1993). Instructional conditions for using dynamic visual displays. *Instructional Science*, 21, 427–449.

Peters, O. (1983). Distance teaching and industrial production: A comparative interpretation in outline. In D. Sewart, D. Keegan & B. Holmberg (Eds.), *Distance education: International perspectives* (95–113). London: Croom Helm.

Piaget, J. (1951). *Introduction à l'épistémologie génétique*. Paris: Presses Universitaires de France.

Piaget, J. (1972). *The psychology of intelligence*. Totowa, NJ: Littlefield Adams.

Piskurich, G.M. (2006). *Rapid Instructional Design: Learning ID Fast and Right*. San Francisco: Pfeiffer.

Power, M. (2008a). The Emergence of Blended Online Learning. *Journal of Online Teaching & Learning*, MERLOT, Volume 4, Number 4, December 15th. http://jolt.merlot.org/

Power, M. (2008b). A Dual-mode University Instructional Design Model for Academic Development. *International Journal for Academic Development.*

Power, M. (2008c). *Le concepteur pédagogique réflexif: un journal de bord.* Athabasca, AB: AU Press. http://www.aupress.ca/books/Michael_Power.php

Power, M. (2007) From Distance Education to E-Learning: a multiple case study on instructional design problems. *E-Learning*, Volume 4, Number 1, pp. 64-78.

Power, M. (2005). Le design pédagogique dans un contexte de bimodalisation de l'enseignement supérieur: une étude multicas. (Instructional systems design at a dual-mode university: a multi-case study). Unpublished doctoral thesis. Québec, QC : Faculté des sciences de l'éducation, Université Laval. Retrieved March 12th 2006 : http://www.theses.ulaval.ca/2005/23258/23258.pdf

Power, M. (1996). La congruence, un principe fondamental dans la planification de l'enseignement. *Actes de Colloque* de l'Association internationale de pédagogie universitaire (AIPU), 9 au 11 août 1995, Université du Québec à Hull, 241–246.

Power, M. (1987). La congruence en enseignement et apprentissage. *Journées pédagogiques.* Libreville, Gabon : Coopération canadienne, CÉGEP St-Jean-sur-Richelieu.

Prégent, R. (1990). *La préparation d'un cours.* Montréal : Éditions de l'École Polytechnique de Montréal.

Prensky, M. (2004). *Digital Game-Based Learning.* New York: McGraw-Hill.

Rieber, L. P. (1994). *Computers, graphics, and learning.* Madison, WI: Brown & Benchmark.

Reigeluth. C.M. (ed.) (1999). *Instructional-design theories and models: A new paradigm of instructional theory, Volume II.* Hillsdale, NJ: Lawrence Erlbaum.

Reiser, R.A. (2001). A History of Instructional Design and Technology: Part II: A History of Instructional Design. *Educational Technology Research and Development* 49 (2), 57-67.

Rumble, G., & Harry, K. (1982). *The distance teaching universities.* London, Canberra & New York: St. Martin's Press.

Sammons, M.C. & Ruth, S. (2007). The invisible professor and the future of virtual faculty. *International Journal of Instructional Technology and Distance Learning*. January, Vol. 3 number 1.

Scallon, G. (1988). *L'évaluation formative des apprentissages 1. La réflexion*. Québec : Presses de l'Université Laval.

Schank, R.C. Berman, T. R. & Macpherson, K. A. (1999). Learning by doing. Reigeluth, C. M. (Ed.) (1999). *Instructional-design theories and models: A new paradigm of instructional theory*. (161–182).

Shale, D. (2002). The hybridisation of higher education in Canada. *International Review of Research in Open and Distance Learning*, 2(2).

Skehan, P. (1998). *A Cognitive Approach to Language Learning*. Oxford Applied Linguistics. Oxford, UK: OUP.

Sullivan-Palincsar, A. (1998) Social constructivist perspectives on teaching and learning. *Annual Review of Psychology*. 49:1, 345–375.

Taylor, J.C., (2001). 5th generation distance education. *DETYA's Higher Education Series*, Report No.40, June.

Tessmer, M., & Wedman, J.F. (1990). A layers-of-necessity instructional development model. *Educational Technology: Research and Development*, 38(2), 77–85.

Tripp, S.D., & Bichelmeyer, B. (1990). Rapid protoyping: An alternative instructional design strategy. *Educational Technology, Research and Development*, 38(1), 31–44.

Twigg, C.A. (2004). Using asynchronous learning in redesign: reaching and retaining the at-risk student. *Journal of Asynchronous Learning Networks*, Volume 8, Issue 1 February.

Visual-Learners.com http://www.visual-learners.com/

Wedemeyer, C.A. (1979). Criteria for constructing a distance education system. *Canadian Journal of Continuing Education*. VI(I), 9–15.

Wedman, J, & Tessmer, M. (1990). Adapting instructional design to project circumstance: The layers of necessity model. *Educational Technology*, 48–52.

Wiley, D. (ed.) (2002). *The Instructional Use of Learning Objects*. Bloomington, IN: Agency for Instructional Technology. Retrieved Oct. 4th, 2008. http://reusability.org/read/

Wilson, B.G. (1996). *Constructivist learning environments: Case studies in instructional design.* Englewood Cliffs, NJ: Educational Technology Publications.

Zemke, R, (1982). *Figuring Things Out: A Trainer's Guide to Needs and Task Analysis.* Reading, MA: Addison-Wesley.

Appendix A

Examples of analogical representations from Power, M. (2008). *Le conseiller pédagogique réflexif: un journal de bord*. Athabasca, AB: Athabasca University Press.)

Concepts de continuité et de rupture
dans l'évolution ....

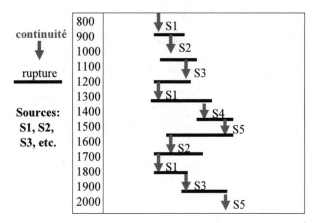

Figure 1: This first representation of the concepts of "continuity and rupture" throughout time (over 1200 years) is rather abstract.

Concepts de continuité et de rupture
dans l'évolution de ....

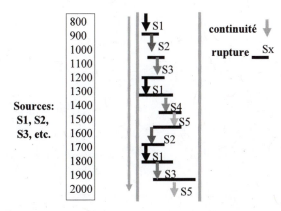

Figure 2: The original analogical representation (Figure 1) was redrawn with colour to better emphasize the "continuity" concept and its juxtaposition with "rupture."

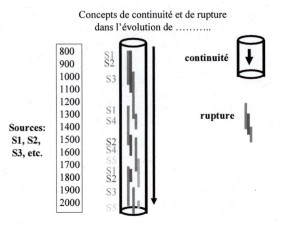

Figure 3: This figure is yet a further evolution of Figures 1 and 2. The analogical nature of the representation (the cylinder) appears here more clearly.

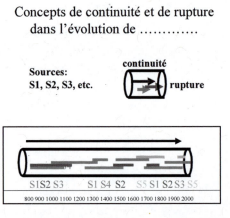

Figure 4: This final figure is but a variation of Figure 3. The horizontal display depicted here was preferred by the faculty member as opposed to the vertical display presented in Figure 3.

Appendix B

"The Congruency Principle": A summary

ORIGINAL TITLE: Congruency: A fundamental principle in instructional design
Michael Power
March 1999

SUMMARY
This article will propose a basic, conceptual model for course design in higher education. It first defines the three functions all faculty members carry out in their work, namely, course planning, course delivery and student performance evaluation. Moreover, using Venn diagrams, these functions are schematized so as to visually demonstrate the importance of establishing a close concordance among all three. This quality of concordance or interrelatedness is termed "congruency." Finally, the consequences of a lack of congruency in higher education will be examined and examples provided.

1. Towards a "congruent" model of teaching
Nowadays, technology is playing an increasingly important role in most sectors of human activity, such as in industry and manufacturing. Nonetheless, in the field of human resources development, human involvement is still considered to be a requisite element, at elementary, intermediary and advanced levels. This can be explained by the fact that an educator's task is, ipso facto, a communicative one as well as one that requires a high level of versatility and flexibility given the variety of learning styles that exist among students. Furthermore, an educator's task becomes more and more complex as learning needs expand, both in terms of quantity and quality. Take, for instance, the following current trends in higher education:

• the number of individuals requiring higher education is continually increasing.

- the quantity of knowledge and skills to be learned is also continually increasing.
- the level of competency (quality) required in the market place is continually increasing as well.

These trends coexistent with yet another one, that of financial limits on budgets allocated by governments to higher education. To sum up, university professors have to educate more and more students, over a longer period of time, to a higher level than ever before, teaching new skills and capabilities to face an information technology-driven job market while having access to lower budgets and fewer means.

In such a context, faculty are required by their institutions to re-evaluate the effectiveness and efficiency of their academic programs in order to take into account these factors. Time-, cost- and effort-saving techniques and strategies have to be developed in order to remain competitive and fully accountable while improving success rates among students. Failure to do so takes on a social dimension and cost since an individual failure eventually translates into a social failure as society in general 'picks up the tab'. Therefore, faculty are increasingly required to demonstrate how their programs fit research-documented and evidence-based needs, meet acknowledged professional norms and, ultimately, can guarantee success. This process of increased expectations on all sides represents, in our view, the advent of nothing less than a new era in higher education on a global scale, the advent of technology-enhanced, cost-effective, learner-based, needs-driven and skills-oriented higher education. In light of the above, this article is an attempt to lay a framework for improved course planning, delivery and student performance evaluation.

1.1 Concept definitions
1.1.1 Function
Every faculty member carries out a number of functions and, to attain efficiency, he or she must harmonize such in order to design, develop and deliver a quality course. In this article, the concept of "function" relates to the three basic tasks that every professor teaching at a university must, to a greater or lesser degree, carry out, namely: course planning, course delivery and student performance evaluation.

1.1.2 Congruency

The term "congruency" is already a well-known concept in the field of educational literature in Quebec (Brien, Nadeau, Girard, Scallon, Morissette, Tousignant, etc.). For instance, in the *Dictionnaire actuel de l'éducation* (Legendre, 1994), it is defined as the correspondence between an attribute and the part of an instrument that is supposed to measure said attribute. It is also defined being a high degree of harmonization between the course goal, general objectives and specific objectives (Morissette, 1984) or between specific objectives and test items (Tousignant, 1985). These definitions are limited however, given the possibility of extrapolating the congruency concept in a more general sense. A new definition of congruency that illustrates the need for continuity and connectedness between a professor's functions will therefore now be proposed.

As was just mentioned, congruency is often defined as a degree of harmony or correspondence between two or more entities, simultaneously. In just this sense, congruency, as defined here, is *the necessary harmonization of all three functions carried out by faculty and aimed at improving learning among students.*

To specialists in educational research who may suggest that the definition proposed with regard to the congruency concept already exists as "validity", such as "content validity" or "construct validity", or even "communality," it may be stated that these concepts are far too limited in scope to describe the concept of congruency as it will be develop here.

2. A professor's functions in light of congruency
2.1 Description of a professor's functions

2.1.1 Course planning: Planning, according to the ADDIE model, involves the process of course design (analysis-design-development-implementation-evaluation) ending in the production and validation of requisite didactic materials. At its very core lies the identification of the essential knowledge, skills and attitudes that will best respond to learner needs. This function requires the elaboration of both course content and form. The three sub-functions inherent in this work are:

• planning course objectives and content (including prior needs assessment)
• planning course delivery (including means and methods).

- planning student evaluation instruments (including assessing learner performance before, during and after instruction).

Course objectives and content planning first involves a front-end, learner-needs assessment analysis followed by the subsequent identification of a course goal and multi-tiered objectives that correspond directly to pre-identified competencies as well as course resource supporting materials (such as Web-based, written, audio or video materials).

Course delivery planning involves elaboration of a teaching strategy which includes the identification of a teaching method while taking into account available means (resources) and thereby adapting existing didactic material or developing new material.

Student performance evaluation planning includes the elaboration of a prerequisites test, a pre-test and a post-test based on choices made during the above course design phases. The development of these instruments as part of the planning function insures, as it shall be demonstrated, a higher degree of congruency with the other two functions.

2.1.2 Course delivery: In chronological order, "course delivery" (actual teaching) is the second function that an educator usually undertakes once his or her planning is complete. During this function, the professor delivers exactly what has been planned in his or her course syllabus, no more, no less. This may seem axiomatic but experience has shown that faculty often stray from set objectives and end up delivering content which does not correspond to set course objectives. Moreover, content delivery must also correspond to the instructional method identified during the planning stage, as set in the syllabus. When done in this fashion, it can be said that delivery is *congruent* with prior planning, i.e. there is absolute, or a relatively high degree of concordance between these two functions. In this sense, one can speak of *course congruency*. Or, in other terms, the more complete the intersection or overlap between functions, the higher the level of congruency.

Figure 1 represents the teaching activity of two professors, one who teaches in a less congruent fashion (Professor A) and one who teaches in a more congruent fashion, Professor B (right), i.e. in that there is a greater level of overlap between his or her planning and teaching. Hence, a lesser level of congruency can be observed for Professor A than for Professor B (right). It can therefore be posited that Professor B has remained more faithful to his syllabus whereas Professor A has likely strayed 'off course', as it were, perhaps pursuing objectives that were not planned or lacking the time management skills necessary to reach the objectives that had been set. The end result is that Professor A's students will likely not reach all the objectives by the end of the course.

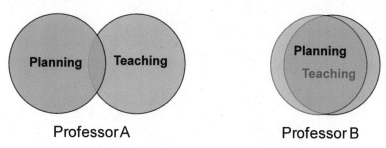

Professor A   Professor B

Figure 1: Congruency between planning and teaching

So as to fully explain what it meant by a lack of congruency, or incongruency, here are two examples of typical situations that sometimes occur.

1) Imagine a history professor who has a special interest in peasant life in the seventeenth century in rural France since this was the subject of his dissertation. Despite the fact that, in his course syllabus, he had only planned to spend a limited number of hours on the subject, he ends up spending twice as much time on it, given his marked interest in the subject. However, by doing so, he necessarily neglects another part of his syllabus.

2) Consider a professor of physical education who is a world renowned specialist in a given sport. Since she excels in this sport, she naturally tends to frequently refer to it and to have her students practice it in her course. However, by doing so, other sports to be taught in her course tend to be either hastily covered or even completely left out.

2.1.3 Learner performance evaluation: The third function carried out by all teachers and professors is learner performance evaluation. If the faculty member has planned his/her evaluation instruments while planning his objectives and content, she or he will already have the requisite means to adequately evaluate his/her students' performance. This function can, in turn, be subdivided into three other categories: *administering a test, correcting it and returning it.*

Linking evaluation to planning and delivery is essential because true congruency cannot exist in a course until such time as it has been successfully achieved. Using the model elaborated above, let's now add this third function to the first two.

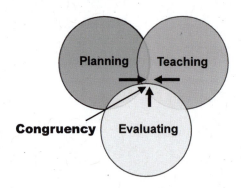

Figure 2: Congruency between planning, delivery and evaluating

In Figure 2, we see that all three functions must tend toward a central position where there is as high a degree as possible of overlap between functions. This occurs when

• what has been planned has been taught and
• what has been planned and taught has been evaluated accordingly.

The likely result is a high degree of congruency. Furthermore, we posit that there is a higher probability of student achievement when high-level congruency has been achieved by a faculty member in a given course, the same applying equally to a program f studies involving numerous professors. This said, we are of course aware of numerous other intervening factors which may alter results, factors such as faculty and student motivation, faculty communicative skills, students perseverance and assiduity, etc. So the congruency principle as presented here looks only at the probable impact of instructional design, teaching practice and student evaluation as conducted by faculty with regard to student performance.

This of course begs the question: what happens when congruency does not occur? What does a professor do after straying away from the syllabus during teaching? Should students be assessed using pre-designed assessment instruments which are based on planned objectives and content or, taking into account actual objectives and content pursued, modify said instruments to bring them in alignment with reality? On the one hand, if their professor assesses their performance based on syllabus-based objectives which have not been achieved or content which has not been covered, one can easily guess the results. On the other hand, if a professor decides to modify the course syllabus and the assessment instruments en route, some unfortunate consequences may ensue. For instance, colleagues who teach subsequent courses in the program and whose job it is to insure program continuity/integrity may have difficulties linking up with these on the spot, undocumented and often uncommunicated syllabus changes.

2.2 Various configurations in function overlapping

We will now turn our attention to an analysis of variations in function overlapping which we believe are fairly typical of situations that arise in higher education. Figure 3 presents three profiles of *incongruency* that can be found in the teaching practices of some faculty members. These variations may seem somewhat extreme but they are being presented to better illustrate the congruency principle and underlying and related problems with regard to student achievement.

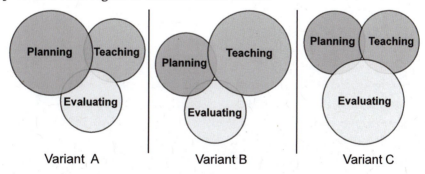

Figure 3: Various configurations in function overlapping (or lack thereof)

Variant A: In variant A, planning appears to be more than ample, the professor having fully designed the course. However, once the course actually begins, the professor appears not to have followed the plan but rather appears to have diverted away from the syllabus to the extent that what is being taught bears little resemblance to what was planned. It should also be noted that what was planned turns out to be more substantial than has been actually taught. Furthermore, what has been evaluated is only partially to what has been planned and to what has been taught. This situation places students in a precarious situation, where they must depend on knowledge acquired elsewhere in order to pass this course.

Variant B: In this case, we observe a professor who appears to be little interested in course planning (or design), being more interested in actual course delivery and expanding on subject matter well beyond the bounds of what was planned. When it comes to evaluation, again we observe that students are disadvantaged in that what is evaluated has little to do with what was planned or actually taught. Such a professor is likely quite spontaneous in the classroom, animating discussions that can take various paths but few which were anticipated. A certain rigour would likely enable this faculty member to help improve the academic results of students.

Variant C is a case of a professor who appears to be overly rigorous in his marking. In actual fact, given the fact that what is being evaluated goes above and beyond what has either been planned or actually taught, severity is simply a disguise for a lack of congruency.

2.3 Congruency on a systemic level
2.3.1 Horizontal Congruency
In light of what has just been examined, it is posited that, should each and every faculty member in a university strive for greater levels of congruency, student achievement would most likely rise markedly whereas absence of any concerted effort to improve congruency would likely result in falling grades and student dropping out. In order to understand how congruency might apply in a systemic way to a group of professors working in the same program, let us look at the following illustration of horizontal congruency." Horizontal congruency occurs when there is an adequate level of congruency in courses taught by a group of faculty in the same program.

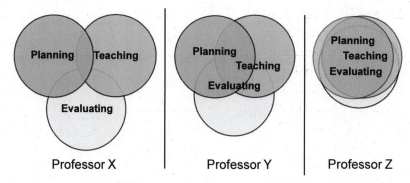

Figure 4 : Horizontal congruency

In this Venn diagram-based illustration, three professors are each offering the same course to three separate groups of students (say Psy 101). It can be observed that Professor X's course has the lowest degree of congruency whereas Professor Y's course is the second-least congruent course. Indeed, in relative terms, a higher level of congruency has been achieved in Professor Y's course when compared to Professor X's course. However, when these two courses are compared to Professor Z's course, they pale in comparison. Indeed Professor Z appears to have achieved almost complete congruency his or her course. As a result, students who happen to be part of Professor Z's class will likely benefit it in their studies in a way that the other students will not, even if they are not the best students at the university. To extrapolate, an average, even weak, student who benefits from congruent teaching over several years may well succeed better than a strong student who, by chance, ended up in classes where the professors lacked congruency in their teaching. The question that comes to mind is: should chance play so great a role in student achievement? Given the issues of student achievement and overall efficiency in higher education as raised at the beginning of this article, shouldn't any factor which might compromise student achievement (such as chance) be removed from out institutions?

2.3.2 Vertical congruency

We will now attempt to demonstrate the consequences of a continuing lack of teaching congruency on student achievement, i.e. on a systemic level.

Imagine a group of students who received instruction which was virtually totally devoid of congruency during their first year of studies but who, during their second year, access more congruent teaching on the part of their professors. Their entry into second year will likely be somewhat arduous given the quality of their instruction in first year and their consequent lack of preparation. Should these students, or most of them succeed in reaching third year and experience an even greater degree of congruency in their professors' teaching, will they be able to make up for lost time and lost opportunity? It is, in our view, altogether plausible that an alarming number of setbacks, failures and even drop outs are directly attributable to incongruency. Figure 5 illustrates the dilemma of just such a group of students as they move from one prerequisite course to the next on their way towards third year and graduation.[1]

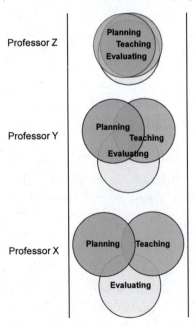

Figure 5: Vertical congruency

In this figure, a rather incongruent path is followed by these students until they reach third year. Of course, despite the difficulties encountered along the way, a good number will graduate regardless of the quality of the teaching received during their studies, benefiting here and there from episodes of congruent teaching, as evidenced by the third year professor. However, one can only imagine the efficiency possible, not to mention academic achievement rates that could be had, were the degree of congruency enhanced among faculty members at all levels and within all groups.

Conclusion

The main objective is writing this article has been to describe gaps in student achievement which may be attributable to a lack of congruency in teaching practice among university faculty using a series of Venn diagrams in the hope that such will provide impetus for change in higher education through an improvement in course quality thanks to improved levels of congruency with regard to faculty teaching functions. We have attempted to indicate some of the consequences, on both individual and collective scales, of a lack of congruency in higher education. We firmly believe that the congruency principle, if applied adequately, will result in improvements in academic achievement among students as well as improved relations between students and faculty.

Bibliography

Bloom, Benjamin. (1979). Caractéristiques individuelles et apprentissages scolaires. (traduit par V. DeLandsheere) Bruxelles: Éditions Labor; Paris: Fernand Nathan.

Brien, Robert. (1990). Éléments de sciences cognitives appliqués à la formation. Québec: Presses de l'Université Laval, Université Laval.

Brien, Robert. (1985). Design pédagogique. Ste-Foy: Éditions St-Yves.

Dick, W. et Carry, L. (1985). The Systematic Design of Instruction. Glenview, Illinois: Scott, Foreman et Co.

Girard, Richard. (1985). La mesure et l'évaluation en enseignement. Québec: Département de Mesure et évaluation, U.L.

Laferrière, Thérèse et Paré, André. (1985). Inventaire des habiletés nécessaires dans l'enseignement au primaire. Ste.-Foy, Québec: Centre d'intégration de la personne de Québec Inc.

Legendre, Reynald.(1994). Dictionnaire actuel de l'éducation. Paris/ Montréal: Larousse.

Morissette, Dominique. (1984). La mesure et l'évaluation en enseignement. Québec: Presses de l'Université Laval.

Morissette, Dominique. (1989). Enseigner des attitudes? Québec: Presses de l'Université Laval.

Nadeau, Marc-André. (1985). Évaluation des programmes. Québec: Presses de l'Université Laval.

Nadeau, Marc-André. (1975) L'évaluation dans la perspective des programmes. Québec: Presses de l'Université Laval.

Paquette, Claude, éd.(1984) Des pratiques évaluatives. Victoriaville, Québec: Editions NHP.

Scallon, Gérard. (1988). L'évaluation formative. Québec: Presses de l'Universté Laval.

Tousignant, Fernand. (1982). Les principes de la mesure et de l'évaluation des apprentissages. St-Jean-sur-Richelieu, Québec: Éditions Préfontaine.

Notes

1. In Quebec, many university programs are three years rather than the four customary elsewhere in North America because students in Quebec go to High School for 5 years rather than6, attending Community College (C.É.G.E.P.) between HS and university.

Appendix C

Examples of teaching activities
© Michael Power 2007

The following is a list of individual and team activities used in distance education and online learning. They were gleaned from various sources, such as learning materials in courses developed at the Télé-Université in Quebec and the Open University in the UK. A number of these types of activities were developed for use in the courses which were the focus of this study.

Algorithmic Design: based on a logical sequence of actions, events, steps, etc. the student is required to draught an algorithm visually setting out the optimal sequence to be followed during an operation, the decision branching points and perhaps acceptable alternatives, etc.

Analogical representations: An activity requiring the student to complete or design a diagram, graphic representation, visual mental model, etc. which may facilitate understanding of abstract concepts, hierarchies, systems, processes, etc.

Analysis: a protocol for the study of text-based documents or excerpts from such based on set parameters, criteria, requirements or categorisations, etc.

Application: after having studied an abstract concept, a strategy or a technique, the student is required to use what s-he has learned by finding a concrete use for it, thereby demonstrating his-her mastery of the learning involved.

Assessment and auto-assessment: the student is provided with an object, a text, or a resource of some kind and is asked to evaluate it according to set parameters or criteria; s-he may also be requested to assess his or her own production using a grid or tool of some kind which is provided or of his or her own making.

Assessment instrument development: an activity that requires that the student demonstrate competency in synthesis, application or assessment;

Categorisation: given access to a data bank or even to a number of odd and even objects or concepts, the student is required to sort them out and establish groups based on shared communalities such as degrees, levels, types, etc.

Comparison: using two or more profiles, situations, case studies, data sets, etc., the student is required to identify similarities;

Creativity: an exercise where the student is left completely free to express himself or herself through the creation of a work of art, an invention, a solution to a problem, etc. using whatever means at his or her disposal, thereby allowing him or her to achieve higher levels of problem-solving, visualisation and cognitive processing.

Decision-making: confronted with a problematic situation, the student is required to analyse, compare, distinguish and select elements which allow him or her to reach a logical and justifiable decision, having weighted the pros and cons within a set timeframe.

Definition: faced with unknown entities (either concrete or abstract), the student is required to define them according to existing standards, protocols, conventions, etc. or to new ones of his or her creation.

Exploration: an activity which can take a number of different directions and, as such, is quite similar to creativity activities. The main difference with this kind of activity is that the student is not always given complete free rein in his-her explorations but, rather, is introduced to, for instance, an author's body of writings, a new environment, virtual or physical, or even a philosophy which has been borrowed from another milieu and applied in a new setting.

Interviewing: the student is requested to select someone to interview based on a set of preset criteria. She or he can ask open-ended or closed-ended questions or a mixture of both in an attempt to unearth new information.

Gaming (educational or 'serious'): activities involving access to, or development of, ludic events, objects or environments, whether real or virtual, for the purpose of learning.

Planning: macroscopic or microscopic development activities based on an event, a production, or some form of achievement. The student must establish a plan of action, identify subsequent steps, set a timetable, using software like MS Project, etc.

Projects: activities which require that the student plan, carry out and report on some kind of a project based on set criteria. This may include events such as a show, a play, a variety hour or an object such as an elaborate child's toy, a playground or a hot rod.

Psychomotor: an activity requiring the student to use his motor skills to achieve an acceptable result, often involving sporting events or team events.

Reflection: an activity requiring the student to become acquainted with a situation, a problem, an event or an issue etc. that needs a period of time for thinking and subsequent discussion. Such activities are often less rigorous than analytical activities sometimes simply resulting in a new procedure or protocol for doing something constructive.

Research / literature review: an intellectual activity requiring the student to undertake a library search for a given thematic or author or problem, etc., in order to develop a systematic and organised databank or data set or collection.

Simulations: activities that allow learners to experience a reality which is dangerous, costly or complicated in a safe, cost-effective and easy-to-access environment.

Story-boarding: activity that requires a learner to write a story while sketching out visual cues to enable the design and development of an educational product, process, production or event.